Praise for *Agents to Agency* and the author

'Most educators would agree that student ownership and agency are essential elements of deep, meaningful student learning. What might not be as apparent, is the pathway to produce these realities. This book creates philosophical and practical clarity for any educator or education system who truly wants to graduate *lifelong* learners. Lee Crockett cuts through the rhetoric and provides insights and practical strategies that have the potential to significantly accelerate student learning.'

> Dr Anthony Muhammad, educational speaker, presenter, and author and co-author of many books including *Transforming School Culture and Professional Learning Communities at Work*® and *High Reliability Schools*

'If students are to become their own teachers, they need the skills, evaluative thinking and opportunities to develop a deep passion for learning. Gaining such agency rarely happens by chance; it needs systematising of the belief that it is important to teach students to become their own teachers and ensuring there is joy in the worthy struggle of this learning. Crockett's Lesson Zero and beyond are powerful methods to enact agency based on the premise there is no perfection, yet it was perfect in the moment that was. O this learning, what a thing it is!'

> John Hattie, laureate professor emeritus at Melbourne Graduate School of Education, The University of Melbourne, and chair of the Australian Institute for Teaching and School Leadership board

'A must-read for every educator. *Agents to Agency* provides the link between our current outdated education system and the "how" to authentically achieve change. It is a book about children and young people at the centre of learning. I highly recommend this book for any educator wanting to shift their practice.'

>   Natalie Otten, Future-Focused Learning executive coach at Evelyn Scott School and president of the Australian School Library Association

'Lee uses his personal journey, his global experience and the literature to shape a seamless and practical argument that we can "do" the fundamentals of learning and teaching differently. If we start with learners and focus on their journeys, we can reframe school experiences, making them relevant and centred on preparing our young people for their futures, not our past.'

>   Professor John Fischetti, pro vice-chancellor of the College of Human and Social Futures, The University of Newcastle

'This book is a must-have for any system, school or educator who has at the heart of their purpose, student agency. Lee Crockett has managed to successfully provide a blueprint for not only the "why" and "what" of student agency but also the "how". *Agents to Agency* recognises where we are at in education and then pushes us to think about what's next in our quest for an education system that truly fosters responsible, capable and independent learners. A concise, clear, practical and important book for any educator committed to self-directed learning.'

>   Gavin Grift, founder and CEO of Grift Education, and author and co-author of books including *Five Ways of Being*, *Collaborative Teams that Work* and the forthcoming *Emerge: The Five Most Common Challenges You Face as a Middle Leader and How to Overcome Them*

'Lee's latest work is a timely reminder that school should not be a place where kids go to watch teachers work. If we learned one thing from the experience of COVID-19 pandemic responses, it is that our learners have great resilience and capabilities. We can include them in the "secret teacher work" and trust them to guide and design their own learning.'

>   Simon Vaughan, principal of Canberra College

'Engagement of learners is so important in our schools, but there are many compelling reasons to move students from an initial position of engagement to something much more powerful and meaningful. It's how we unlock the capacity of a community of inquiry and practice to go from the transaction of interaction to the transformation of permission. In *Agents to Agency*, Lee Crockett skilfully sets out a practical blueprint to support educators with the necessary "how" for equipping, empowering and enabling young people to transform their own lives through amplifying learner voice, agency and advocacy in our schools and, ultimately, society.'

> Adriano Di Prato, educator, former deputy principal, co-founder of a School for tomorrow. and co-author of *Game Changers: Leading Today's Learning for Tomorrow's World*

'I am such a fan of the brilliant writing and work of Lee Crockett. In *Agents to Agency*, Crockett provides an illustrative roadmap of "destinations, milestones and footsteps" with exceptional clarity for developing student agency over their learning. I have planted his Lesson Zero flag into all of our mathematics lesson design work. The book offers a brilliant, practical and precise rationale, structure and process for us to follow.'

> Dr Timothy D Kanold, award-winning educator, author of books including *HEART!* and *SOUL!*, and former superintendent of Adlai E. Stevenson High School District 125, a Model PLC at Work® district in Lincolnshire, Illinois

AGENTS to Agency

A measurable process for cultivating self-directed learner agency

Lee Crockett

 A catalogue record for this book is available from the National Library of Australia

Cover Design: Lee Crockett

Designer: Matthew Harrod

Editor: Alissa Voss

© 2023 Future Focused Learning Network

Published by Wabisabi Learning Inc. All rights reserved.

This work is copyright. Apart from fair dealings for the purposes of study, research, criticism or review, or as permitted under the Copyright Act 1968 (Cth), no part should be reproduced, transmitted, communicated or recorded, in any form or by any means, without the prior written permission of the copyright owner.

#117–5525 West Boulevard
Vancouver, BC, Canada
V6M 3W6

ISBN: 978-1-7380531-0-0

Acknowledgements

In Zen it is understood that consciousness does not belong to us. Like the air we share, consciousness is a collective resource and impossible for an individual to claim. Such it is with this book; the influences that formed it are countless. How can one sum up all the experiences and people that have shaped one's life? As other educators and I seek to improve ourselves and remove barriers to success for learners, we collectively cleanse the mental environment that all of us share and have inherited.

There are a few mentions of gratitude I wish to share. Firstly to Kathleen Baker-Brown and Ross Crockett, who have made immeasurable contributions to this work. They constantly challenge my thinking and elevate my game. To Simon and Jackie Vaughan, for their extensive support. To the countless teachers and school leaders worldwide who have embraced my work and the thousands in the Future-Focused Learning Network who have challenged themselves with the masterclasses. It is their evidence that I share and their success that I celebrate in this book.

To the Rinzai Zen community in Japan, particularly Tokozenji in Yokohama, Kenninji in Kyoto and Engakuji in Kamakura, for their gracious acceptance. To Diago Ozawa, for patiently helping me to again find the path when it was lost. To Lenzan Kudo, for the playful breathing. Lastly to Kaori Yoshida, for being an unwavering source of sunshine and joy.

Table of Contents

Acknowledgements vii

About the Author xi

Introduction 1

Chapter 1: What is Agency and Why Does it Matter? 11

Chapter 2: Learning Intentions 2.0 29

Chapter 3: Purposeful Questioning 49

Chapter 4: Lesson Zero 65

Chapter 5: Destinations, Milestones and Footsteps 83

Chapter 6: Progressions to Self-Directed Learner Agency 101

Conclusion 127

References 131

Index 137

About the Author

Lee Crockett is an optimist. He believes in a bright future and our ability to build it together through connection and compassion. He works with governments, education systems, international agencies and corporations to help people and organisations connect to their highest purpose and realise their wishes for the future.

Lee believes in creating balance in the reality of a digital present and future. As such, living in Kamakura, Japan, he studies Zen and the shakuhachi, a traditional Japanese bamboo flute. Mindfulness and joyful curiosity are the foundations of his approach to creating vital learning environments for groups worldwide.

His several bestselling books, including *Future-Focused Learning*, *Literacy Is Not Enough*, *Growing Global Digital Citizens* and *Mindful Assessment*, have garnered many awards and are used in schools and universities around the world.

To learn more about Lee's work, visit leecrockett.net.

Introduction

I have always had a passion for learning. As a child I would disassemble everything from radios to bicycles to figure out how they worked. I took things apart and built new things through what I had learned. Unfortunately, though I loved learning, I *hated* school.

In Canada, high school spans three years, encompassing Years 10 through 12. In my Year 10 physics class, I became restless as the teacher worked through the textbook from the beginning. A few weeks in, I recognised the pattern: we worked through the book's examples and the teacher assigned the exercises as homework. My teacher confirmed this was the case and that the textbook spanned the physics curriculum for the next three years. For the first time in my school life, I had access to what we would be learning and how I would know I was successful.

I could not have been happier and began working through the text, following the examples and explanations, and doing the exercises and practice tests. Eventually I encountered problems where the mathematics was too complex, so I began working my own way through the mathematics textbooks. In this manner I learned all the high school mathematics, including calculus, to further my physics studies. I would go to the university library on the weekends to read and learn more. By the end of my first year of high school, I had independently completed both the physics and mathematics curriculams for Years 10 through 12.

The problem began when it came time to choose courses for the following year. I knew I required Year 12 physics and mathematics, but not Year 11, for university entrance, so I registered for Year 12 classes. This, of course, raised a flag and resulted in a meeting with the principal, who explained that even though my grades were excellent, I had not completed the Year 11 levels. I argued that I had completed the Year 11 and 12 material, and some university-level work as well, on my own while the teacher crawled through the Year 10 curriculum.

To prove my capacity, I asked to sit the final exams for Year 11 and even proposed that if I scored less than 90 per cent I would gladly sit through an additional year of instruction. Such a concept did not exist back then, and the principal explained that he had no authority to approve that plan. When pressed, he said only the Minister of Education could make that decision.

Naturally, the next day I skipped school and went to the legislature to track down the Minister. I sat outside his office without an appointment until he agreed to meet with me. I explained the situation and pleaded my case to challenge exams. He refused, stating there was no way I could know the subject unless I had taken the class. At that moment I realised school had no meaning for me. As a result, despite my love of learning, determination and hopes to go on to university, I dropped out of high school. I had come to the realisation that school as I experienced it was a prison for the mind, focused more on checklists of things to be taught than being a place and an opportunity to actually enable learning, and therefore it was of no purpose to me.

The Problem: The Pedagogy of Oppression

While my experience, particularly my decision to drop out, may be exceptional, I have learned through my work with schools worldwide that thousands of students feel similarly imprisoned in their learning by the very institution that is supposed to encourage it. From requiring students to use method A to solve a problem instead of method B, even if the results are the same, to mandating that students sit in classes for a specified number of hours per subject each week, regardless of learning level, the education system imposes seemingly arbitrary conditions in almost all facets of the student learning experience. In its current iteration, school appears to be authoritarian, hierarchical, bureaucratic and alienating (Farmer, 2020; Florkowski et al., 2022; Stoddart, 2021). Some scholars even point out that the discipline of individuals was school's original purpose (Blishen, 1969). Forcing learners to sit and be taught and to conform to the system's arbitrary requirements for learning, at a time when technology has enabled students to access the sum total of existing knowledge with a click of a button, could not be more futile. The students in our classrooms have access to anything they want to learn. So why do governments mandate that they sit in classes? Why should there be a requirement for how many hours a student spends in a classroom in addition to a performance requirement? I could continue with countless examples, and I am sure you have your own as well. Instead, let me simply state that this unyielding, authoritarian approach – *the pedagogy of the oppressed*, a term originally coined by Paulo Freire (1970) – has to end if we are to create capable, independent learners equipped to thrive in their future.

Though the aim of school has shifted in the past several decades to the development of individuals (Vallance, 1974), what remains is the struggle to realise the democratisation of education – that is to say, the assurance of learners retaining a significant level of ownership for the direction, methodologies and assessments of the learning they are expected to undertake. Since the 1970s, multiple global and societal changes, including rapid socioeconomic change, new communication technologies, rising unemployment and the evolution of learning theories, have led to the modern-day need to redirect our structures from teaching to learning (Marbeau, 1976). It is clear that a change from teacher-centred and content-focused methods is needed to prepare students to succeed in the modern world. Some schools have recognised this and are already making changes. But change for mere change's sake is not enough, and it is not effective. Teachers are exhausted from change fatigue and direction *du jour*. In conversation, teachers have even said openly to me that they often avoid the current change initiative, keep their heads down and avoid eye contact until the principal goes to another conference and comes back with a new change initiative. The key to success is recognising where one's practice is currently and implementing transparent, measurable processes to evolve it to a clearly defined and established end point.

The Peril of Hoping

In the years leading to the global pandemic, governments and education policymakers made a dramatic shift, putting student agency at the centre of the conversation. In Victoria, Australia, the Department of Education's

Agents to Agency

Amplify strategy highlights 'empowering students through voice, agency and leadership' as its most urgent priority (State of Victoria Department of Education and Training, 2019, p. 1).

In Canberra, Australia, the Australian Capital Territory (ACT) Education Directorate's Future of Education (FoE) strategy goes further, placing student agency at the program's centre. The strategy focuses on learners making decisions about their learning and how their learning environments operate, and on teachers recognising that each student treads their educational pathway based on their developing interests, knowledge and skills. The Directorate states:

> Respecting the human agency of a child requires that students are active participants in their learning, making informed choices about what and how they learn, contributing to decisions about how their learning environment operates. (ACT Education Directorate, 2018, p. 4).

The FoE's phase 2 implementation plan defines the success of the initiative as:

> Ensuring children and young people are engaged in their learning by taking a holistic view of their unique needs and interests, respecting that they are active participants in their learning who can make informed choices about what and how they learn. This includes a focus on connection, belonging, inclusion, cultural integrity, and personalised learning. (ACT Education Directorate, 2022, p. 3)

Unfortunately, I am concerned that these worthy initiatives are likely to fail as no process exists with which to achieve the outcomes. Instead, it is left to schools, hoping they will figure out a way. Hope is not a strategy; it is a wish. There is little hope without a measurable, transparent process across the spectrum of diverse needs from kindergarten to postsecondary levels (Ladson-Billings, 2011). Further, without a consistent, quantifiable approach, every aspect of the initiative, from the methods to the outcomes, will vary widely from school to school, ultimately impacting the learners and creating a further disparity in the school system.

The FoE First Phase Implementation Evaluation Report, written three years after the initiative began, provides little evidence in support of its goals.

Evaluation is measured through student-reported behavioural and emotional engagement and perceptions of teacher support for learning. The report defines *behavioural engagement* as 'how intensely a student tries their best' and includes self-reported levels of hard work, active participation and effort (ACT Educational Directorate, 2021, p. 6). The *emotional engagement* domain includes concepts such as 'students enjoying the work they do in class' and 'their perceptions of how much fun learning in class is' (ACT Educational Directorate, 2021, p. 6). The *academic emphasis* domain measures student perceptions of 'the extent to which teachers encourage independent thinking, give extra help, set high standards and want every student to work hard and to do their best' (ACT Educational Directorate, 2021, p. 6). There is a profound disconnect between these measurements and the initial goals of 'making informed choices about what and how they learn, contributing to decisions about how their learning environment operates' (ACT Education Directorate, 2018, p. 4). Students may work hard, have fun in their classes and feel like their teachers want them to work hard, but these are ineffective indicators of learner agency.

> *Hope is not a strategy; it is a wish. There is little hope without a measurable transparent process across the spectrum of diverse needs from kindergarten to postsecondary levels.*

Agency is an outcome of self-direction, evidenced by individuals taking the initiative to diagnose their learning needs, formulate their learning goals, identify appropriate resources, choose and implement learning strategies and self-evaluate their learning outcomes (Knowles, 1970). All these things can be measured to provide a better picture of achieving learner agency, and this book will show you how.

A Chance for Change: The Shift to Learner Agency

My decision to drop out of high school was, fortunately, not the end of the story but only the beginning. One dedicated industrial arts teacher, who was thoroughly committed to my future, showed up at my home one Saturday and started helping me rebuild a carburettor. Eventually he guided the conversation back to school and, although he knew I had no intention of going back, asked me to return. He had arranged with all my teachers that I had only to show up for exams. As long as I was performing well, I could spend my time in the industrial arts campus learning whatever I wanted. On Monday I was back in school.

I asked my teacher what I should do and he explained he had classes and couldn't teach me, so I should just pick something to learn and learn it. I devoured every book and machine I could get my hands on. I learned printing, photography, photo editing, drafting, circuit design, programming, electronics, graphic design and more. My teacher refused to teach me anything but would answer if I came to him with well-formulated, specific questions along with an explanation of why I was asking the question and what I had done to answer it on my own first. It was the first time in a school environment that a teacher got out of the way and let me learn. That year I completed the entire high school industrial arts curriculum and passed my exams in all other subjects.

I share this story because it is the perfect example of agency. It's not that I was brilliant, just incredibly curious and determined. All I needed to truly engage in learning was the knowledge of what I wanted to learn and how I would know I was successful. I needed a teacher to point me towards that and then get out of the way. Nowadays, most of the professional learning work I do with schools is about guiding teachers to get out of the way of learning. I believe teaching – if done with the focus on the teacher – may be the most significant impediment to learning. If done with the focus on the learner, it may be learning's greatest catalyst.

The COVID-19 pandemic was a stern awakening for education in that the dialogue regarding changes in education, which had remained the same for decades, was no longer optional. Schools were thrown into chaos trying to prepare for the near-global suspension of face-to-face instruction. Data from the United Nations Educational, Scientific and Cultural Organization (UNESCO) report on COVID-19 Education Response shows that on 15 April 2020, 195 countrywide school closures affected 1 581 100 422 learners, which was 90.3 per cent of total enrolled learners globally (UNESCO Institute for Statistics, n.d.).

Notwithstanding the circumstances causing the lockdown, I must admit that I was excited about the possibility for methodological change that I was certain the turn to remote learning demanded of the

Introduction

education system. In the crucible of lockdowns, without the availability of traditional, face-to-face teaching methods, schools would finally have to do something different. In these circumstances, I observed schools taking two different approaches.

First, some schools regressed to even stricter authoritarian practices. Even when learning moved online, primarily occurring via Zoom video calls, the educators at these schools seemed to want to continue talking at students synchronously. Nothing had really changed in the teaching methods; the students were simply online for classes. The result was a disaster – students failed to show up to classes; those who did turn up were late and left their cameras switched off, so it wasn't clear if they were even paying attention; others had problems logging in or handling software. Because of this, teachers spent much of their time holding sessions to reteach or re-explain what they had already taught during the main lesson. This method was time-intensive for educators while achieving dubious results with students. It was not remote learning, but online teaching; an attempt to continue the pedagogy of the oppressed without the physical controls.

Other schools we worked with, however, seized the opportunity to radically challenge their previously undisrupted systems. Instead of expecting learners to show up and listen at a specific time, teachers recorded lessons, which allows learners to review at a time of their choosing. This also allows for pausing to reflect, note-taking and watching certain sections over again. These recordings were more an example of provocation than simple content delivery and included relevant challenges for learners to undertake, which required learners to research and discover many things on their own. Meeting time then evolved into a rich conversation, where the learners did the majority of the talking and the teacher posed questions and facilitated conversation. Learners were not only responsible for their learning but also for constructing success criteria as well as creating and presenting their evidence of learning.

This was an easy model for these schools as it was the same approach they experienced in my masterclasses in the Future-Focused Learning Network. I am very clear that synchronous time should be used for rich discussion, creating clarity and cultivating deep understandings. These schools were able to transition in and out of remote learning with minimal stress because there was little difference in how they worked in both scenarios. In fact, teachers at Lalor Primary School remarked near the end of the lockdown that they had been so effective during remote learning they wanted to ensure they did not regress their practice.

If we learned anything from two years of remote learning, it is that synchronous delivery of content should rarely happen and that learners must be able to direct their learning. This shift – moving away from the pedagogy of oppression to the pedagogy of agency – is what will produce functional, independent learners who know how to learn, how to capture evidence and document their learning, and how to recognise what success looks like.

The Structure and Use of This Book

Since the publication of *Future-Focused Learning: 10 Essential Shifts of Everyday Practice* (Crockett, 2019), masterclasses for each shift have been implemented in schools worldwide through the Future-Focused Learning Network (available at futurefocusedlearning.net). Within each shift, a continuum from *agents of the teacher* to *learners with agency* guides the transformation of classroom practice, moving the responsibility for learning from the teacher to the learner. This book picks up where *Future-Focused Learning* left off; it takes a deeper look at the transition from agents to agency and how to achieve it successfully.

Synchronous delivery of content should rarely happen, and learners must be able to direct their learning.

Agents to Agency explores how to adopt learning practices that develop and enhance learner agency and will provide the understanding you need to move forward in your classroom. In the following pages, I urge you to approach what you will come to know about agency with an open mind and heart. There is no question that educators want their learners to succeed in and out of the classroom. Ultimately, however, our purpose as educators is to ensure that once our children leave school, they are responsible, capable and independent learners. Our learners must become their own educators and thought leaders, and the emergence of agency in our classrooms is a significant facet of providing this direction.

Introduction

Chapter 1 breaks down what agency is and discusses why it is essential to successful, meaningful learning. From there, Chapter 2 explores the crucial topic of learning intentions and success criteria, and Chapter 3 reveals the process of purposeful questioning. These understandings are fundamental as you move into Chapter 4, which reveals Lesson Zero, an approach to providing agency that puts what you learned in Chapter 2 at the forefront of your practice. In Chapter 5 I present the topics of destinations, milestones and footsteps, which are essential for plotting lesson trajectories, measuring success and promoting learner accountability. Finally, Chapter 6 presents a series of learner agency continuums for facilitating and measuring learner agency as sensible and practical progressions for building self-directed learner agency with your learners. At the end of the book are case studies and an invitation to join the Future-Focused Learning Network to provide you with ongoing support in your quest to help students move from agents to agency.

Chapter 1

What is Agency and Why Does it Matter?

Everything that is really great and inspiring is created by the individual who can labour in freedom.

Albert Einstein, *Out of My Later Years*

In *Pedagogy of the Oppressed* Paulo Friere (1970) explains how education can be an instrument of oppression to the voice of the individual. Oppression begins with our education system and curriculum, which has authoritarian rule over the dissemination of knowledge by what the government or individual educators permit to be taught. A pedagogy of oppression tells a student 'what to think with respect to values, attitudes, and beliefs, the very heart of what determines the uniqueness of the individual' (Hase & Blaschke, 2021, p. 5).

Hase and Blaschke (2021) make a strong case for agency by stating:

> From an educational point of view, there is a commonly held belief that it is up to others (the educators) to make sense of the world for the learner, and that knowledge is tightly held in the hands of the educator. It is the pedagogy of the oppressed. It is a belief that belongs to an era when information and knowledge were difficult to obtain, and codification was left in the hands of

those who had access to that information and knowledge – initially religion and later the educational system. Freedom from this pedagogy of oppression thus requires a pedagogy of agency. (p. 6)

Like literacy, agency is not pedagogy or a subject; it is an outcome ...

While education has demonstrably been oppressive in the past, it can also be liberating, unshackling us from thoughts dictated by others, guiding us to establish our values and beliefs and developing our understanding of the work by fostering agency and forming our meanings through our experiences as envisioned by great thinkers such as Dewey (1986) and Piaget (1971). This chapter presents agency as a solution to the pedagogy of oppression, discussing both the history of agency in education as well as the teacher's role before clarifying some misconceptions surrounding the concept of agency.

Agency in Education

Agency is the antithesis of oppression. Like literacy, agency is not pedagogy or a subject; it is an outcome of an education system that places autonomy, individual development, self-determination and self-direction at the foundation. Knowles (1970) defines *self-direction* as:

> The process in which individuals take the initiative, with or without the help of others, in diagnosing their learning needs, formulating learning goals, identifying human and material resources for learning, choosing and implementing learning strategies, and evaluating learning outcomes. (p. 7)

Agency describes the ability to identify valued goals and desired outcomes and to proactively, purposefully and effectively pursue those goals and outcomes (Chuter, 2020). This includes mindful reflection on one's values and priorities, a conviction of self-efficacy (Bandura et al., 1999) and the capacity to act intentionally towards specific goals (Locke & Latham, 1990). Agency is a blend of mindfulness, intention and action. From the perspective of Zen, mindfulness is living and doing, always in reality, with simplicity and neutrality.

Learning is the process by which we acquire new understandings, knowledge, behaviours, values, skills, attitudes and preferences (Gross,

2020). The experience of learning is personally empowering. It enables people to make sense of the world around them on their terms instead of those dictated by others. Research suggests it also fosters a sense of agency, with 'the learner making decisions about learning, from what will be learned and how, to whether learning has been achieved and to what degree' (Blaschke et al., 2021, p. 6). But what does this actually look like in the classroom environment?

When we consider the way schools have operated traditionally, it would appear, on the surface at least, that providing learner agency has not historically been a priority for most educators. This idea goes back to the establishment of our first educational institutions. Historically, schooling was provided by a teacher who was to serve as the marshal of knowledge, only dispensing what was necessary for students to evolve their learning to meet the requirements of the next topic, the following unit or the subsequent examination.

For the most part, traditional modes of organising educational environments dictated that learning was strictly regimented and undertaken in a primarily linear trajectory, the earliest schools having been modelled after the factories and assembly lines of the 1800s and 1900s (Jukes et al., 2010). One can surmise this simply by observing the structure of a traditional classroom, which appears quite linear in nature. In such a learning environment, the teacher becomes the focus as the disseminator of information within what educator Tony Bates (2015) describes as 'a predominantly factory model of educational design, which largely remains our default design model even today' (p. 81). The notion of learner agency directly challenges the very structure of schools and classrooms as they are today and have existed for centuries.

The Role of the Teacher

During my work with educators and in delivering keynotes internationally, I habitually ask the following question:

> Who is responsible for the learning in your classroom and school?

Pause for just a few moments and consider what your response might be. When I ask this question, it often provokes some heated discussion. Is it the teachers, the administration, the learners or the parents? If it is perhaps some combination of them all, I would further ask what percentage to assign to each and why. Now, put aside that question and take a moment to ponder this:

Who is responsible for the learning in your life?

> *This purpose of school must not be the passive consumption of random knowledge but instead learning how to learn.*

The answer is obvious: you are responsible for the learning in your life. It would be difficult to argue that your learning is anyone else's responsibility. As adults functioning in the world outside school, you and I are accountable for what we learn and how we learn; we have complete self-directional command and agency over our learning and can choose the best ways of building knowledge for ourselves. And when it comes to our employers, business partners, team members and even our spouses and children, this is what is expected of us.

If this is the kind of learner we need to be as independent adults, when and how will we learn to be so? Why should it be any different when we are students in school? Is school not the perfect place and opportunity to develop this? The purpose of school must not be the passive consumption of random knowledge but instead learning how to learn.

Take a moment to reflect on your experience as a young student. When were you most engaged in learning? At what times did you feel like you were hearing and talking about things that truly mattered to you? What was it about education that impacted you the most? Can you pinpoint those precise moments where you connected with the topics on far more than a base intellectual level? Chances are this was in those moments you were free to experience your way of learning and were engaged in practices that connected to your interests. In short, you were likely acting as a self-governing agent of your education.

Fast-forward to the present and think about the students in your classroom. Imagine having learners who, instead of waiting expectantly to internalise input before taking any learning initiative, know what to do and how to move the momentum of their education forward. Envision a learner who asks sensible and meaningful questions and, more often

What is Agency and Why Does it Matter?

than not, answers them independently. Develop a picture in your mind of groups of learners working together enthusiastically, challenging each other in their quest to solve problems that truly matter to them and the world. Imagine learners who comprehend the need for learning and have a heartfelt passion for it. That is the ultimate purpose of fostering learner agency – the development of responsible, capable and independent learners. I ask you to challenge yourself with this question: Are your learners agents of the teacher, or do they have agency over their learning?

The ultimate purpose of fostering learner agency is the development of responsible, capable, and independent learners.

Agency transforms learning from passive consumption of random knowledge into high-level engagement in which the student becomes the leader of the learning. Agency is about personalisation and efficiency for achieving outcomes mutually determined by both the teacher and the learner while building the learner's confidence and capacity through self-direction and self-reflection.

Through agency, learners maintain curiosity and commitment because they now have a stake in their education that may not have been there previously. As a result, agency motivates students to learn and empowers learners to take ownership of their learning and provide meaningful contributions to their learning environments (Organization for Economic Co-operation and Development [OECD], 2019). Other improvements in a learner's educational experiences when given agency over learning include increased confidence, a renewed interest in learning, higher engagement and increased willingness to learn (Reeve & Tseng, 2011). This engagement that is a by-product of agency also ensures, as one study stresses, that 'students will be empowered to take ownership of their learning, to make purposeful contributions to their learning environments, and to tackle issues arising in the world around them' (State of Victoria Department of Education and Training, 2019, p. 7).

Are your learners agents of the teacher, or do they have agency over their learning?

You would be hard pressed to find any intellectual or emotional magic pill that will ensure engagement in the modern classroom. However, shifting agency for the learning to our learners may be a crucial step in ensuring that engagement because in the hands of our learners is where learning belongs. It is their learning; therefore they, the learners, are ultimately responsible. As I state in *Mindful Assessment*, 'Teachers do not create learning; only learners create learning' (Crockett & Churches, 2017, p. 2).

Instead, the teacher's role in the modern classroom is to introduce and facilitate learning pathways. It is the students who ultimately must walk those paths and experience what is on the way, and providing agency is the key to helping them tread those pathways with joy and success. We should not see learning as the outcome of teaching but rather allow teaching to become a mindful response to learning (Crockett & Churches, 2017).

Agency is a skill for both learning and life, and it is indeed both learnable and able to be constantly refined throughout one's life (Mameli et al., 2018). Although the term *agency* is often used interchangeably with other terms, such as *autonomy*, *voice* or *responsibility* (which we will look at in more detail later in this chapter), it is so much more than these things combined. Agency can be viewed as a way not only of learning but also of being in the world.

Teacher Agents Versus Learner Agency

The terms most often used to define *agency* are many and varied (Vaughn, 2020), and this book has already discussed some compelling interpretations of agency in preceding sections. When it comes to classroom learning, however, probably the most straightforward terms are best, so I will continue by saying that I believe agency means having autonomy over learning.

Autonomy is defined as 'the quality or state of being self-governing' and 'self-directing freedom and especially moral independence' (Merriam-Webster, n.d.). In modern classrooms, learners possess agency over their learning if they can intervene in and transform established educational practices using their individual actions or words (Mäkitalo, 2016).

The learners in our classrooms are unique in that they each possess talents and interests that span a broad range of areas. Such facilities allow them to participate actively in life to enrich their personalities, contribute to the societies they are a part of and honour the cultures they represent. Agency recognises that 'each student treads their educational pathway based on their developing interests, knowledge and skills' (ACT Education Directorate, 2018, p. 4).

According to the Amplify study (State of Victoria Department of Education and Training, 2019), agency means that learners:

- work with teachers in making decisions about teaching and learning
- take responsibility for their learning and are, on the whole, independent and self-regulating learners
- negotiate and design learning that stretches their thinking
- can track and measure their learning growth
- are involved in designing and implementing school policy and programs and actively contribute ideas about student-led learning
- display the capabilities, confidence and willingness to contribute ideas and make decisions about what and how they learn
- reflect, take action and accept the responsibility that comes with being part of the problem solving. (p. 23)

Figure 1.1 demonstrates the fundamental differences in learning between the learner acting as an agent of the teacher and the learner having agency over the learning.

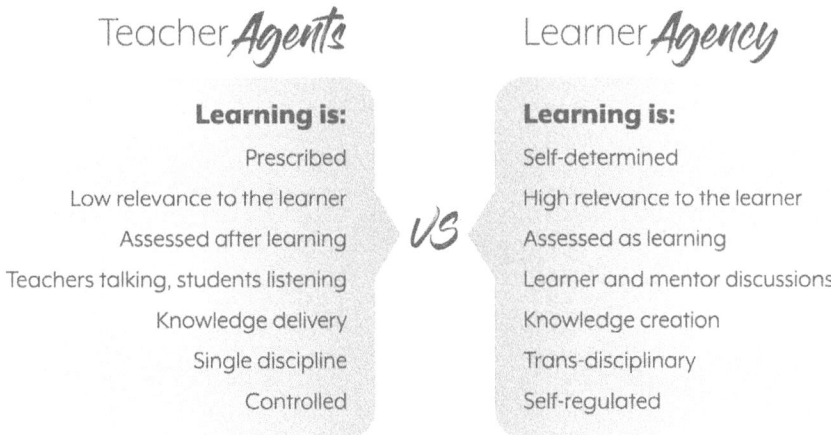

Figure 1.1: The fundamental differences in educational experiences between learners as teacher agents versus learners with agency over learning.

In figure 1.1 (page 17) we see that the pursuit of agency ensures that learning remains student-centred and is predominantly designed, directed, revised and even assessed by the learners. The more the control, choice and pace of learning remain in the hands of the teacher, the less agency learners have over their learning.

Making student agency the focal point in education means first permitting and ensuring students become active participants in their learning, then releasing the responsibility for their learning. As such, we must equip them with the skills for making informed choices about the direction and method of that learning and making decisions regarding how their learning environments operate (ACT Education Directorate, 2018). Along the way we nurture their talents and abilities while maintaining agency and independence as central themes in their learning.

Misconceptions About Agency

There are plenty of misconceptions surrounding the concept of agency, and it is essential to address these and gain an awareness of them.

Agency Is Different to Responsibility and Voice

As we explore the meaning and importance of learners having this agency in learning, it may be helpful to discuss a few terms agency is often confused or used synonymously with. One is the *responsibility* for learning, and another is the *learner voice* concept.

Let's begin with responsibility. According to one study, 'the concept of gradual release of responsibility does entail building student capacity to voice their views and opinions, to collaborate, and to lead themselves and others' (State of Victoria Department of Education and Training, 2019, p. 20). The same study goes on to define the role responsibility plays for learners in leadership roles, which includes a capacity for actively listening to and clarifying the issues of the peers for whom they advocate and modelling strong leadership practices and ethics for the same, all of which serve to develop trust and autonomy among the learner collective.

Though responsibility and agency may seem almost the same and are certainly related, they differ in the sense that responsibility can be said to fall under the broader umbrella of learner agency. As with a finely-tuned machine, responsibility is an integral facet of agency, and agency would not be a complete experience with it absent, but it is not agency in itself. Instead agency 'reveals the attitude to transform situated practices through words and actions', whereas responsibility 'outlines the subjective feeling of self-regulation and internal commitment' (Mameli et al., 2018, p. 43).

According to the OECD Learning Compass 2030, agency implies that responsibility is an integral factor as students participate in society to influence people and events for the better. Agency also requires the capacity to devise an overall purpose for guiding action and thought, and identify steps and milestones to achieve a goal (OECD, 2019).

The same document also stresses that agency means acting, not being acted on; shaping rather than being shaped; and making individual choices and conclusions instead of merely accepting those of others (OECD, 2019). The shift from acting instead of being acted on and making conclusions instead of accepting the conclusions of others is the shift from a pedagogy of oppression to a pedagogy of agency. In other words, learners shift from being agents of the teacher to having agency over their learning. Another point worth considering is that agency in any learner's role or process in an educational endeavour may be regarded as complementary to, but distinct from, having responsibility for their learning (Carpenter & Pease, 2013).

When we observe the concept of agency alongside responsibility – which has to do with obligation, accountability and personal commitment – it is easy to see how the state of ultimately practising agency over one's affairs, especially one's learning, requires a measure of responsibility for its success. It is, however, much more than just responsibility itself.

Then there is the matter of voice. Rather than being simply about communicating ideas and opinions, voice lends learners a certain capacity to effect change (State of Victoria Department of Education and Training, 2019). However, agency and voice are quite different because, as with responsibility, voice could be considered one facet of the broader concept of agency. To explore this difference, all one needs to do is consider who is in a position of control in the case of voice versus agency.

With voice, students have input but no control over decisions. Their opinions are heard and shared, providing insight into the direction learning could or should take for the highest benefit of all, but the final decision is still out of their hands. However, with agency learners are autonomous and in complete control when it comes to learning.

Because of the confusion around these terms, I offer this straightforward definition to help align our thinking: if learners have *voice*, they have a *vote*; if they have *agency*, they have *autonomy*.

Although related, the terms *voice* and *responsibility* are not interchangeable with *agency*. Learner agency is more than simply the freedom to learn as one will. It includes but is certainly not limited to exercising full responsibility and accountability for having autonomy, demonstrating a fair and level-headed use of one's voice and being willing to adapt and respond as learning evolves proactively.

Agency Does Not Mean Alone

Each learner passing through our classrooms today and in the future who is given agency over learning will journey along a very personal educational pathway. Their developing interests, knowledge and skills will define their journey and develop their attitudes, values and beliefs. However, agency does not mean the student acts exclusively alone. Agency is also not about acting solely in self-interest. While agency does provide a certain level of individual freedom, teacher facilitation in the classroom is still critical to the process. In essence, agency aims to ensure that students build autonomous skills in concert with their teacher's support and guidance to achieve mutually determined outcomes.

If learners have voice, *they have a* vote; *if they have* agency, *they have* autonomy.

Further, today's modern learners thrive on interaction and collaboration with their peers, and agency as both an individual and a team member are significant aspects of learner success. This is a concept I refer to as *collaboration fluency* (Crockett & Churches, 2017). A learner doesn't develop agency independently; for the most part, agency works well when thought of as a co-agency involving family members, peers, teachers and the wider community over a lifetime (OECD, 2019; Schoon, 2018). In this way, learners receive support in pursuing their learning goals and developing agentic independence from a network of individuals who know how to achieve these things and can guide them accordingly. Agency truly is a process of interconnecting with and relating to others.

Agency Is Not Just for Older Students

When we discuss the concept of agency – of students becoming leaders of their own learning and essentially *learning how to learn* – it is easy to think that such a process should only be applied after students have arrived at a certain age or developed particular higher-order skills. However, this could not be further from the truth.

One of the resources I have created and shared in the Future-Focused Learning Network is Bloom's zoonomy. It uses different animals to reinforce the concepts of the different levels of Bloom's taxonomy, and it is loved by younger learners. For example, the elephant is the symbol for remembering because everyone knows elephants never forget! Learners at Evelyn Scott School in Canberra begin with the zoonomy in the Early Years program and by Year 1, the learners have an excellent understanding of Bloom's levels and are able to create their own success criteria. Figure 1.2 (page 22) is the work of Year 1 students presented with the learning intention 'Learners recognise how strengths and weaknesses contribute to identities'. This is a standard pulled straight from the Australian Curriculum achievement standards and has not been rewritten in student-friendly language. As I will discuss in Chapter 2, there is much value in unpacking the learning intention with the learner, and it provides an incredible opportunity for developing literacy at very high levels. After unpacking the learning intention, learners then co-construct success criteria against levels of Bloom's. Not only does this ensure they understand the learning intention, it also provides them with a range of opportunities to present evidence of learning, all of which demonstrate success.

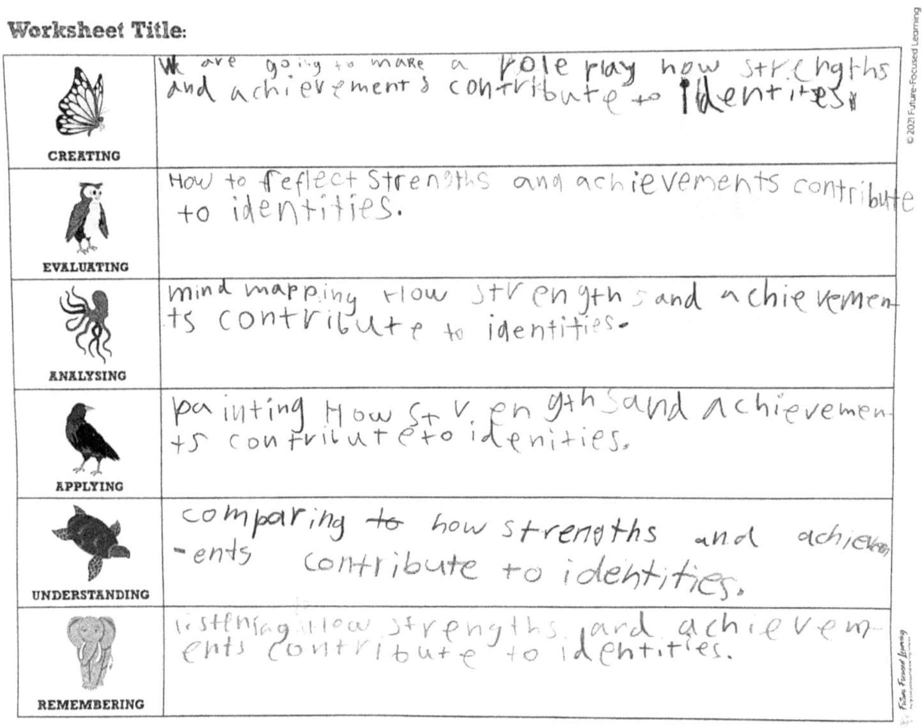

Worksheet Title:		
CREATING	We are going to make a role play how strengths and achievements contribute to identities.	
EVALUATING	How to reflect strengths and achievements contribute to identities.	
ANALYSING	mind mapping How strengths and achievements contribute to identities.	
APPLYING	painting How strengths and achievements contribute to identities.	
UNDERSTANDING	comparing to how strengths and achievements contribute to identities.	
REMEMBERING	listening How strengths and achievements contribute to identities.	

Source: © 2022 by Evelyn Scott School. Used with permission.

Figure 1.2: Year 1 learners at Evelyn Scott School construct success criteria against levels of Bloom's zoonomy.

Consider for a moment an impact of this. Learners are able to, with guidance, unpack an achievement standard at an adult language level and then independently build success criteria in multiple variations aligned to Bloom's. If they are capable of this at Year 1, how well will they tolerate the pedagogy of the oppressed at middle or high school? In fact, as Year 1 learners are doing this now, there is absolutely no reason older leaners should not be doing the same. Further, we must reconsider what, if any, direct instruction should be happening at senior levels.

Why Agency Matters

Since the world moved online decades ago, we have seen a monumental shift in not only how we live but also how we communicate, how we do business and especially how we learn. The globalisation, automation and digitisation of multiple industries have transformed the work landscape in the modern world. For example, the work performed by those in low-skill occupations, such as labourers, machine operators, drivers and clerical workers, is becoming increasingly automated (Grainger et al., 2018), and thus the need for such workers is decreasing.

In light of this, the workforce looks different because it requires a completely updated and more robust set of capabilities. The present and future learners in our education systems will be filling occupations those of us living today have never heard of and solving problems of which we cannot even conceive. This supports a sentiment I shared over a decade ago in the book *Literacy Is Not Enough*:

> To stay competitive in this new global economy, we need to shift our instructional approach to a learning environment that will provide our students with the most in-demand skills; those that can't be easily outsourced, automated, or turned into software: creativity, lateral thinking, and problem solving dealing with non-routine cognitive tasks. (Crockett et al., 2011, p. 11)

Historically, occupations often required workers to be adept in specialised content knowledge to be able to perform their roles. Nowadays content knowledge is almost ubiquitous; information is easily and quickly accessible, with the workforce having instantaneous access to the total of human knowledge in the palms of their hands (Crockett et al., 2011). As a result, although there are exceptions, jobs are often less about what the worker knows in a particular moment than about how they can access that knowledge and arrive at the correct answer. Thus, the skills students need are less to do with memorising content and more to do with learning how to learn what they need to know, when and how they want.

According to one study, today's learners now need the capacity for enterprise, creativity, collaboration and teamwork (both in person and remote), problem-solving and digital literacy skills as well as curiosity, courage, resilience and the capacity to be self-motivated, independent workers and learners (Richardson & Mishra, 2018; Voogt et al., 2013). While forcing a single perspective on learning presents a barrier to the development of such skills (Blaschke et al., 2021), giving learners agency can facilitate their growth and prepare students for the modern workforce.

As educators, we must recognise the need for students to foster lifelong learning skills and the capabilities therein, which include but are not limited to:

- critical thinking capacity
- creativity
- problem-solving ability
- ethical and moral considerations
- intercultural awareness and understanding
- personal responsibility
- social skills.

Cross-disciplinary competencies like these are part of a child's continuing development as a lifelong learner. In the practice of agency in designing, crafting and assessing their learning, learners can attain, hone and demonstrate these skills throughout and beyond their formative years. If we wish for our learners to foster these skills to the point where they are fluent and the skills have become second nature, I believe that we must bring the pursuit of providing learner agency to the forefront of our teaching practices.

Teacher Facilitation of Agency

According to educator Margaret Vaughn (2019), a classroom that prioritises the development of a learner's agency produces educational experiences that leave out the traditional transactional approach of learning, shifting to one that is co-constructed and more conducive to improving independent problem-solving and building critical thinking capacity. Through agency, learners can develop a self-perception based on their capacity for independent thought (Williams, 2017). As teachers, the idea is not to tell learners what to think but to guide them in understanding how they can think. We do this by using mindful assessment techniques and reflecting to the students what we observe as they practise agency. By receiving this feedback, they heighten their abilities as independent critical thinkers who construct their understandings from what they learn (Williams, 2017). Learning can happen using structured, semi-structured and unstructured methods, and providing learners with opportunities for agency seeks to remove, as much as possible, any barriers to students taking advantage of any combination of these methods.

There is a significant variance of agency across K–12, distinguishable by observing the amount of agency a learner receives when their formative years first begin in kindergarten and comparing this to what they encounter as they move into postsecondary education. I would argue that the amount of agency learners are given decreases as year levels progress. As curricular content becomes increasingly complex, teachers tend to take more responsibility in the higher grades by creating units, structuring lesson delivery, designing assessments, marking assessments and so forth. In *Future-Focused Learning*, I assert that 'as learners move through the school system, teachers take on more and more responsibility, and we departmentalise and compartmentalise the learning' (Crockett, 2019, p. 93). I go on to explain what the ideal scenario would be for a senior school environment:

> I believe one of education's primary goals is to create competent, independent learners, and most educators would probably agree. If this is the case, then the easiest teaching job in the school system should be the high school teacher that works with senior-level students. By this point, those learners should be approaching the benchmark of functional, independent learning and only require minor support. However, it seems the opposite is true. (Crockett, 2019, p. 93)

Learners have little to no agency over their learning by the time they are in high school and preparing to move to postsecondary studies. The problem with this is that, should they decide to move on to university or other further study, after a three-month break they will be expected by their postsecondary instructors to suddenly be entirely self-directed learners with complete accountability for their learning, even though they have spent the previous twelve years having opportunities for refining that exact capability systematically withheld. It is a strange expectation for us to place on our learners, and in my opinion it makes the case for ensuring learners gain and retain agency throughout their learning careers even stronger.

Agents to Agency

We must shift responsibility for learning from the teacher, where it has been, to the learner, where it should be. Agency is an authentic, real-world way of approaching this shift. The real world doesn't have neat compartments or set disciplines for success; it demands adaptability, patience and a willingness to learn and use the acquired knowledge in the moment. Most of all, it requires us to take full responsibility for what we learn, how we learn and how we choose to use that knowledge within our lives. For our learners to be successful, that is the shift in ownership that needs to happen, and it is what learner agency encourages.

We must shift responsibility for learning from the teacher, where it has been, to the learner, where it should be.

Summary and Key Points

- Agency is about learners having autonomy over their learning, not about learners doing whatever they want.

- The point of agency is to develop responsible, capable, independent learners.

- Agency is about personalisation and efficiency to achieve mutually determined outcomes while building confidence and capacity through self-regulation and self-reflection.

- The practice of developing learner agency hasn't been a priority in education, and as year levels increase, learner agency becomes less apparent in a learner's experiences.

- Learner agency can develop many crucial life skills within learners, including critical thinking capacity, creativity and problem-solving ability.

Guiding Questions

1. What does it mean to have agency in learning?

2. In your days as a student, when do you feel you experienced a sense of agency over your learning?

3. What is different about how learning is conducted between when teachers act as agents and when learners have agency?

4. What are some of the misconceptions that are common about learner agency?

5. How do the terms *responsibility*, *voice* and *agency* differ, and how are they related?

6. How does making the shift to giving learners agency over learning help them in life beyond school?

Chapter 2

Learning Intentions 2.0

And let us not forget that even one book, one pen, one child and one teacher can change the world.

Malala Yousafzai, Inauguration of the Library of Birmingham, January 2013

To become successful with agency, learners must understand what they are learning, why they are learning and how they will know they are successful. For that to happen, firstly, as educators, we must thoroughly understand what our students are learning, why they are learning it and how we will know they are successful. Secondly, we must make this abundantly clear for our learners, beginning with precisely what they are learning, as no learning journey can begin without establishing a point of origin. Even more common among learners than the questions about *what* they are learning, however, are inquiries relating to the *why* of learning. In school, learners always wonder, 'Why are we learning this? What is the purpose here? When will I use this in the real world?' As I emphasise in *Future-Focused Learning*, 'to learn something, it must stimulate your curiosity – in other words, interest precedes learning' (Crockett, 2019, p. 21).

Why they are learning something is a fair question for learners to ask since they are the ones being expected to learn. Additionally, it is essential that they have a clear set of criteria to help them determine if they have been successful. These things collectively define the essence of *learning intentions* and the success criteria attached to them. That is what learning intentions are – the what, why and how of learning. Unfortunately, there is much confusion around learning intentions and success criteria. This chapter aims to create a shared understanding of their language and processes.

The Intentions of Learning

At the very least, we should be able to agree as educators that every one of us wants to accomplish something significant with our learners. Our curriculum is built around intentions, and we walk into our classes with a purpose: to see our learners succeed. The question is, how do we accomplish that? How do we get there? How will we help them in that process? To do so effectively, we need to think about the intentions of learning and what we are trying to achieve to arrive at that journey's end. In other words, we need to ensure our learners know where they are going and how they will know they have arrived at the destination. It seems such a simple and obvious thing to say, but it is essential to understand. What obstructs us from reaching this goal is that we do not traditionally share our intentions and criteria for success, thereby hiding from our learners that ultimate destination.

Often in the past, teachers have kept curriculum documents to themselves and not shared them with students. However, the shift to making curricula transparent represents a significant step towards advancing learner agency. When students obtain clearly stated goals and guidance through shared learning intentions and success criteria, the effect on both the learner and the learning itself can be significant (National Council for Curriculum and Assessment, 2015). Nevertheless, as learners progress to higher grades in the school system, it seems like the teacher assumes more and more responsibility for learning as they exclusively unpack the curriculum, design the lessons, build the assessments and create the examinations, all without input or insights from the ones doing the learning. I assume many teachers take this on themselves by choice, but so doing runs counter to the whole idea of fostering in our students a sense of agency and guiding them to being capable, independent learners by the time their school years have concluded. Further, operating in such a manner conflicts with our expectation that students must achieve such independence within an education system, as the system itself is unclear on how to scaffold it.

To be effective and to promote learner agency, the learning experiences we craft for our learners must contain clear learning intentions and specific criteria that clarify what a learner's success looks like. Doing so helps learners understand and commit to their learning goals and provides them with appropriate challenges that will lead them to successful learning (State of Victoria Department of Education and Training, 2017). Clearly and explicitly sharing with our learners precisely what they are learning and how they will know they have learned it provides a foundation for a productive educational experience and effective assessment of learning (UK Department for Education and Skills, 2007). In fact, without teachers providing a comprehensive awareness to learners regarding both the learning intentions and success criteria, as John Hattie (2012) claims, learners 'are hardly likely to develop good assessment of that learning' (p. 47). Proper learning intentions should not only provide an effective means of formative assessment but also facilitate the utilisation of consistent, ongoing feedback to fill the gaps between a student's current and new knowledge (Snow, 2022).

As our students' learning careers advance, our mission should be to enable them to the point where they no longer need us when they leave us for good (Crockett, 2019). We can accomplish this by demonstrating to them the importance of a clear understanding of learning intentions – in other words, knowing where you are going, how you will get there and how you will know you have arrived.

In addition, we can help them set goals, and we explore this subject further in Chapter 5 (page 3). For the time being, it is worth mentioning that setting goals involves determining a particular standard or objective as the aim of one's actions (Schunk, 2001). Establishing personal learning goals can positively affect academic performance as many learners discover through self-reflection that studying is part of the pathway to achieving personal, relevant life goals (Schippers et al., 2020). In the case of learning intentions, the success criteria reflect the goals learners must strive to reach. As teachers discuss and unpack learning intentions with their students, the students can determine personal goals regarding the criteria for success, perhaps placing them in their own words for better comprehension. Progressing towards these goals allows learners to practise agency and maintain motivation by comparing their performance with their goals through self-assessment (Schunk, 2001).

Learning Intentions and Lesson Objectives

All learning needs both a purpose and an objective. Knowing the destination and the purpose for learning keeps your learners on track, providing a clear picture of the goals they are meant to reach and why they are essential (Crockett, 2019). However, there is a critical distinction we need to make clear moving forward: the difference between *learning intentions* and *lesson objectives*.

When discussing a learning intention, it is important to realise the intention itself is essentially a statement that describes in clear language what students are intended to ultimately know, understand and accomplish as a result of learning and teaching activities (National Council for Curriculum and Assessment, 2015). Learning intentions are the essential understandings, critical concepts and individual perspectives we want learners to embrace.

Essential Understandings

An essential understanding shapes our learners' identities, personalities, ethics, belief systems and moral compasses. They are the primary intention behind the learning, and they ask us to consider what curricular elements we want to bring forward and how those would shape our learners. Essential understandings encourage learners to think deeply about what's relevant to them, what they believe and what they disagree with. In the case of the Australian Curriculum, the three most effective locations from which to source your essential understandings are:

1. **Learning Area Rationales:** Here you will find the big ideas and critical concepts you want your learners to grasp. As you teach, you must consider what core concepts and acknowledgements you are striving to have your learners embrace and bring into their lives. You'll find these in the rationales. For example, an essential understanding pulled from the learning area rationale for Year 7 humanities and social science (HASS) might be:

    Thinking about and responding to issues requires an understanding of different perspectives; the key historical, geographical, political, economic and societal factors involved; and how these different factors interrelate.

2. **Year Level Descriptors:** All year level descriptors reveal specifically what key concepts and inquiries define the essence of a certain area of learning, which can be seen in this example from Year 7 media arts:

    We make personal evaluations of our own and others' artworks by exploring meaning and interpretation, elements and forms, and social and cultural contexts.

3. **General Capabilities:** If you look around, the general capabilities are filled with potential for essential understandings. The achievement standards we use are drawn from the general capabilities, and these categories represent a well-rounded, conscientious and responsible citizen. This is what makes it a prime source for obtaining essential understandings. Consider this example extracted from the general capabilities learning area Intercultural Understanding:

    Intercultural understanding involves learning the value of our own culture, languages and beliefs, as well as those of others.

Critical Concepts

Critical concepts are the crucial points of knowledge we want our learners to comprehend and internalise. To fully comprehend an essential understanding, there are usually critical concepts of which we must obtain an appreciation and a humble understanding. I say *humble* because if we truly realise what these concepts are, then the result is developing an understanding that they are often lifetime journeys of learning by themselves. The potential depth of the learning hidden within critical concepts is quite significant, and it's where we have the capacity to create transformative learning experiences. Consider the following example from Year 3 HASS:

- **Learning Intention:** Learners identify the importance of different celebrations and commemorations for different groups. They explain how and why people participate in and contribute to their communities.

- **Essential Understanding:** The greatness of our community can be found in its diversity.

- **Critical Concepts:** Greatness, community, diversity.

Individual Perspectives

Individual perspectives connect learners to the intention using their unique experiences, thoughts and opinions as well as those of others. Individual perspectives represent both a connection to our learners and their thoughts, but also the search for different voices, stories and opinions in our learning. The purpose of exploring individual perspectives is to encourage learners to *inquire* – to share what they know and think already, and what they're curious about. One of the most effective ways we can unpack individual perspectives is through using purposeful questions (which we'll address in greater detail in Chapter 3, page 49) and having conversations with our learners about their ideas, what they might be curious about, or what prior knowledge they might have to bring to the learning. Here is an example using a learning intention from Early Years English:

Learning intentions are the essential understandings, critical concepts and individual perspectives we want learners to embrace.

- **Learning Intention:** Identify connections between texts and personal experience.
- **Purposeful Questions:** Has this ever happened to you? What is most interesting about this? Which is your favourite part and why? Can you write, draw or tell your own story about your experience? Is this book like something else you've read?

Learning Intentions Versus Lesson Objectives

Though related, learning intentions and lesson objectives are distinctly different. Learning intentions describe the concepts and understandings we want learners to learn and internalise. Lesson objectives contain the various tasks and activities that will drive the learning for our learners. In other words, learning intentions are about learning, and lesson objectives are about doing. More specifically, lesson objectives are what we are doing to achieve the learning intentions.

Learning intentions are consistently confused with lesson objectives. As such, teachers might believe they are addressing learning intentions when in fact they are only responding to the necessity for having tasks for their learners to perform over the course of the lesson.

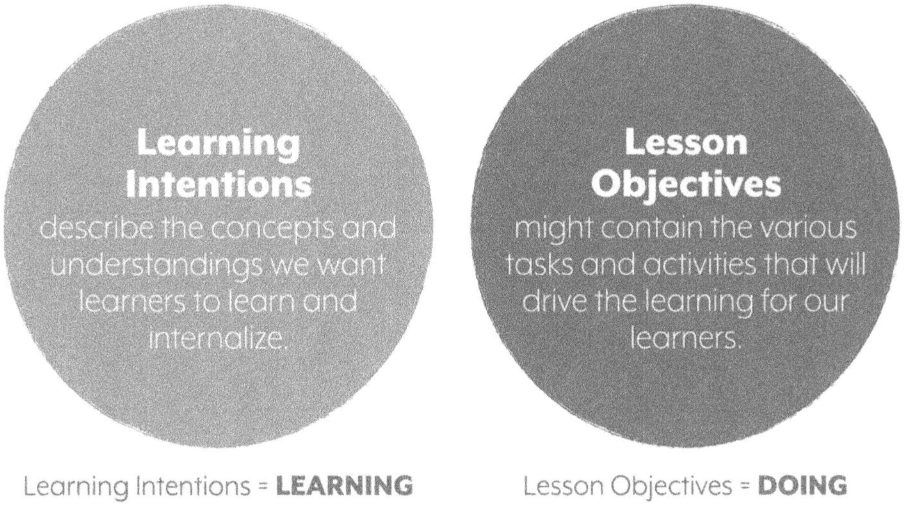

Learning Intentions 2.0

Learning Intentions — describe the concepts and understandings we want learners to learn and internalize.

Lesson Objectives — might contain the various tasks and activities that will drive the learning for our learners.

Learning Intentions = **LEARNING**   Lesson Objectives = **DOING**

Figure 2.1: Regarding learning, intentions and objectives are two distinctly different things.

As an example, a pair of teaching tools often used in classrooms over the last few decades are the acronyms WALT (We are learning to) and WILF (What I am looking for), which are attributed to educator Shirley Clarke (Ralph, 2019). In practice, the teacher sets clear expectations by defining WALT and WILF at the beginning of a lesson, ensuring students understand the lesson's objectives and content (State of Victoria Department of Education and Training, 2017). Though WALT is often equated with learning intentions, it generally refers to the intended lesson objectives or tasks. WILF, though identified as success criteria, is related to task completion.

The issue with WALT and WILF is that they are not representative of the broader concepts and understandings of learning. Instead they focus on what students are doing *in the lesson*, making them more akin to lesson objectives. The WALT and WILF approaches address learning pursuits within a specified time, usually a class period or two, and as such are more indicative of short-term tasks or objectives. Learning does not fit within a specified period; it takes as long as it takes for the individual. Thus, neither WALT nor WILF accurately identify the learning intentions for a given lesson.

Learning does not fit within a specified period; it takes as long as it takes for the individual.

Again, learning intentions are the essential understandings, critical concepts and individual perspectives, all of which are timeless and extensive. As with an essential question, learning intentions are less about finding a definitive answer and more about developing a deeper understanding and appreciation for what is to be learned. Figures 2.2–2.5 display the Learning Intentions Shift of Practice from Early Years to Year 10 in the Future-Focused Learning Network.

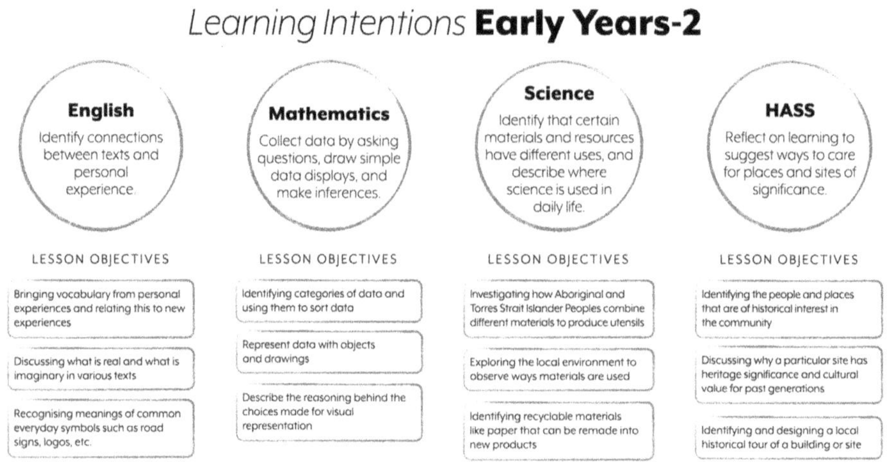

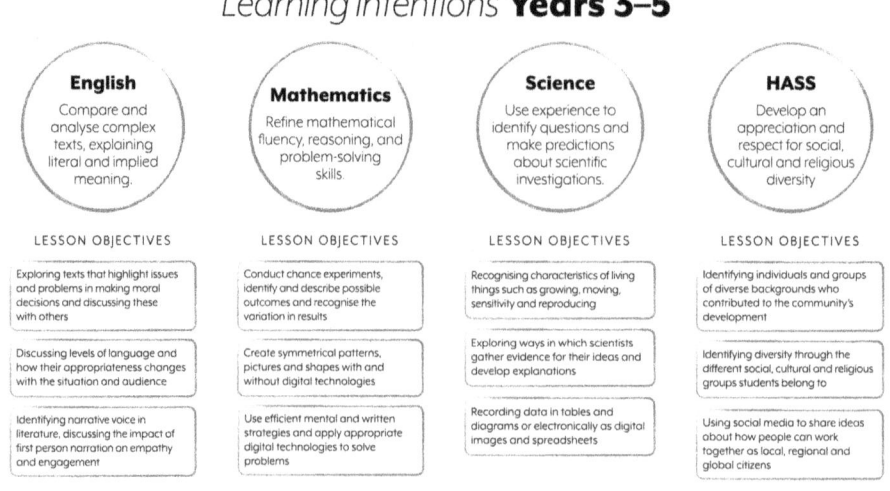

Source: © 2022 by Lee Crockett, Future-Focused Learning Network.
Figure 2.2: Learning intentions for Early Years–Year 2.

Source: © 2022 by Lee Crockett, Future-Focused Learning Network.
Figure 2.3: Learning intentions for Years 3–5.

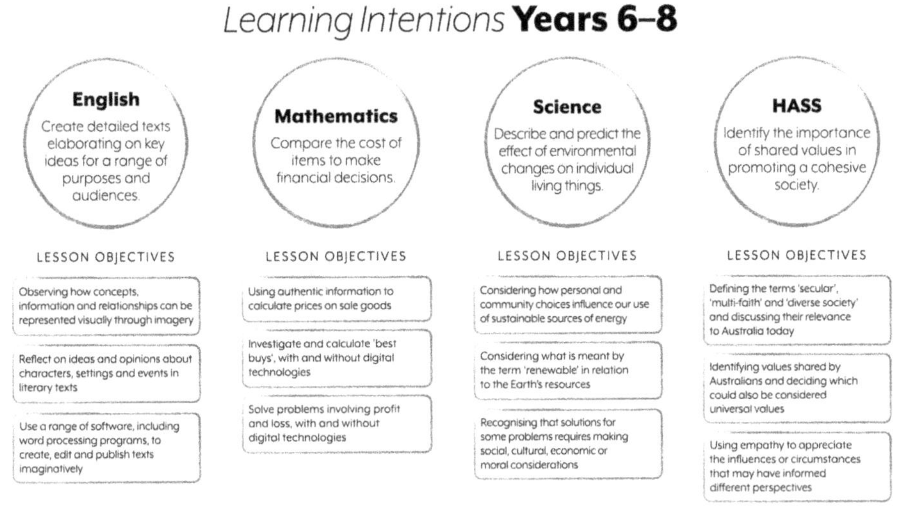

Learning Intentions Years 6–8

English
Create detailed texts elaborating on key ideas for a range of purposes and audiences.

LESSON OBJECTIVES
- Observing how concepts, information and relationships can be represented visually through imagery
- Reflect on ideas and opinions about characters, settings and events in literary texts
- Use a range of software, including word processing programs, to create, edit and publish texts imaginatively

Mathematics
Compare the cost of items to make financial decisions.

LESSON OBJECTIVES
- Using authentic information to calculate prices on sale goods
- Investigate and calculate 'best buys', with and without digital technologies
- Solve problems involving profit and loss, with and without digital technologies

Science
Describe and predict the effect of environmental changes on individual living things.

LESSON OBJECTIVES
- Considering how personal and community choices influence our use of sustainable sources of energy
- Considering what is meant by the term 'renewable' in relation to the Earth's resources
- Recognising that solutions for some problems requires making social, cultural, economic or moral considerations

HASS
Identify the importance of shared values in promoting a cohesive society.

LESSON OBJECTIVES
- Defining the terms 'secular', 'multi-faith' and 'diverse society' and discussing their relevance to Australia today
- Identifying values shared by Australians and deciding which could also be considered universal values
- Using empathy to appreciate the influences or circumstances that may have informed different perspectives

Source: © 2022 by Lee Crockett, Future-Focused Learning Network.

Figure 2.4: Learning intentions for Years 6–8.

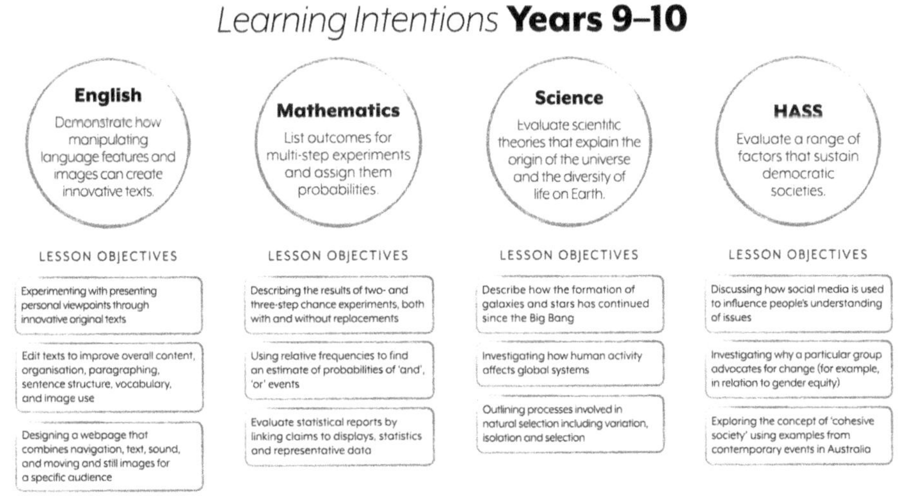

Learning Intentions Years 9–10

English
Demonstrate how manipulating language features and images can create innovative texts.

LESSON OBJECTIVES
- Experimenting with presenting personal viewpoints through innovative original texts
- Edit texts to improve overall content, organisation, paragraphing, sentence structure, vocabulary, and image use
- Designing a webpage that combines navigation, text, sound, and moving and still images for a specific audience

Mathematics
List outcomes for multi-step experiments and assign them probabilities.

LESSON OBJECTIVES
- Describing the results of two- and three-step chance experiments, both with and without replacements
- Using relative frequencies to find an estimate of probabilities of 'and', 'or' events
- Evaluate statistical reports by linking claims to displays, statistics and representative data

Science
Evaluate scientific theories that explain the origin of the universe and the diversity of life on Earth.

LESSON OBJECTIVES
- Describe how the formation of galaxies and stars has continued since the Big Bang
- Investigating how human activity affects global systems
- Outlining processes involved in natural selection including variation, isolation and selection

HASS
Evaluate a range of factors that sustain democratic societies.

LESSON OBJECTIVES
- Discussing how social media is used to influence people's understanding of issues
- Investigating why a particular group advocates for change (for example, in relation to gender equity)
- Exploring the concept of 'cohesive society' using examples from contemporary events in Australia

Source: © 2022 by Lee Crockett, Future-Focused Learning Network.

Figure 2.5: Learning intentions for Years 9–10.

Once we have identified our learning intentions, our role is to communicate them to our students. As we unpack a learning intention with our students, we can create meaningful questions about the concepts they contain to engage our learners in connecting to and building on them in ways they find interesting and relevant. However, the conversations we have around unpacking a learning intention with learners take time to bear fruit. It is a process that absolutely cannot be rushed. Exploring a learning intention effectively spans a more extended period than simply an individual lesson. It is impossible to unpack a learning intention in the first few minutes of a lesson and then expect it to be completed by the lesson's end. This should reinforce the importance of understanding the difference between a learning intention, which spans days, weeks or even months, and a lesson objective, which is what learners do in the allotted block of time.

Learning intentions are less about finding a definitive answer and more about developing a deeper understanding and appreciation.

A study done at the University of Glasgow (Crichton & McDaid, 2016) involved asking both teachers and learners from junior to senior year levels in schools in West Scotland about the efficacy of learning intentions and success criteria. While the learners' responses were overwhelmingly positive, their complaints were primarily focused on the lack of time teachers spent with them on discussion and clarification. It seemed that every teacher in the study merely complied with the discussion of intentions and criteria for the purposes of the study but did so as quickly as possible so they could get right to what they felt was the actual objective of the class – their planned lesson (Crichton & McDaid, 2016). Unfortunately, it seems this desire to jump directly to the teaching without a discussion of what the expectations and goals were or how both learner and teacher would know the learner had reached those goals left learners confused and frustrated about their lack of understanding of the learning intentions and success criteria. To learn effectively and gain agency over the learning, learners should feel involved in their learning through a shared understanding of and commitment to learning intentions and success criteria with their teachers (Snow, 2022).

Learners should feel involved in their learning through a shared understanding of and commitment to learning intentions and success criteria.

Clarity: The Shortest Distance to Successful Outcomes

As discussed, learning intentions are the understandings and realisations that sprout from our learning. They are defined by what learners are meant to learn, not what we want them to do during class. Essentially, a learning intention done well gives learners total clarity about what they are learning, why they are learning and how they'll know they've been successful (Crockett, 2019). How does this expedite our learners arriving at the projected learning outcomes we've established together?

First, let us establish what *clarity* means, especially regarding learning. To me, clarity means freedom from illusion and delusion, a crucial consideration for us to make when it comes to learning intentions and, indeed, when it comes to the whole process of learning. It is a lucidity of perception and understanding that eliminates indistinctness and ambiguity.

Let's look at this from an occupational standpoint and consider collaboration as it applies to the average workplace. According to one study, employees who 'work as teams with a specific team goal, rather than as individuals with only individual goals, increase productivity … Furthermore, the combination of compatible group and individual goals is more effective than either individual or group goals alone' (Lunenburg, 2011, p. 4). In my experience working with schools and businesses worldwide, teams do their most profound and most creative work when they are unified by a clarity of purpose, plan and responsibility. I often suggest such clarity be adopted as an operational norm simply because teams with collective clarity know precisely what is to be done and by whom, even if they are operating remotely from one another or have different areas of responsibility. Having this kind of clarity not only produces stellar work in record time but is also a great system of maintaining teamwide accountability.

In terms of education, the point to take away from this is that *clarity facilitates learning*. Suppose learners are not clear regarding where they are going or how to get there. In that case, it is challenging for them to arrive, particularly since we are discussing agency as something we want learners to exercise independently. The more time learners spend traversing the muddy waters of vague intention and ill-defined success criteria, the farther away they get from achieving our expected outcomes.

Clarity means helping learners identify what they need to learn and how they will know they have learned it. When students know more about these things, they learn more effectively (Fisher et al., 2018), and evidence of this can be seen clearly in John Hattie's (2008) work on effect sizes, which are statistical measures of how profound an impact a specific educational influence or intervention has on learning. For example, an effect size of 1.0 is associated with the advancement of learners' achievement by one school year, or an improvement in the rate of learning by approximately 50 per cent. According to Hattie (2008), teacher clarification of learning intentions and success criteria has an effect size of 0.75. This should make abundantly clear the importance and impact of investing the time to do this well and not rushing the process to get to the learning; effectively and thoroughly unpacking learning intentions and establishing mutually determined success criteria is the learning.

Our minds can fashion every misperception or misunderstanding imaginable when we don't see the road ahead. We can conjure ambiguous notions about how the whole scenario will play out, which is precisely what happens to our learners. We must help our learners understand the destinations for their learning – our learning intentions – and that we provide them with the tools to remove ambiguity. That is how we will support learners to arrive at those destinations quickly and successfully.

Learning as a Connected Journey of Intentions

The curriculum is rarely a random bit of learning; rather, it is consistently part of a much more significant concept that is scaffolded over time. In other words, learning is a journey rather than a destination. It is about constantly connecting our interests, experiences and especially prior learning to build knowledge and insights we can use throughout our lives.

All learning has a point of origin and becomes more valuable by building on what came before it. The resource learners have when beginning a new learning challenge is their prior knowledge. The construction of newer knowledge and more profound interest requires building on what has come before it (Ferlazzo, 2020). A fundamental question for learners to ponder at the origin of learning is what they already know that is useful and how they know it, followed by considering how they can extend it.

The knowledge of our past, present and future learning is connected on any educational journey. When we look at the learning intentions for any learning area or level, we can quickly identify both past and future learning intentions, all of which are linked together (see figure 2.6).

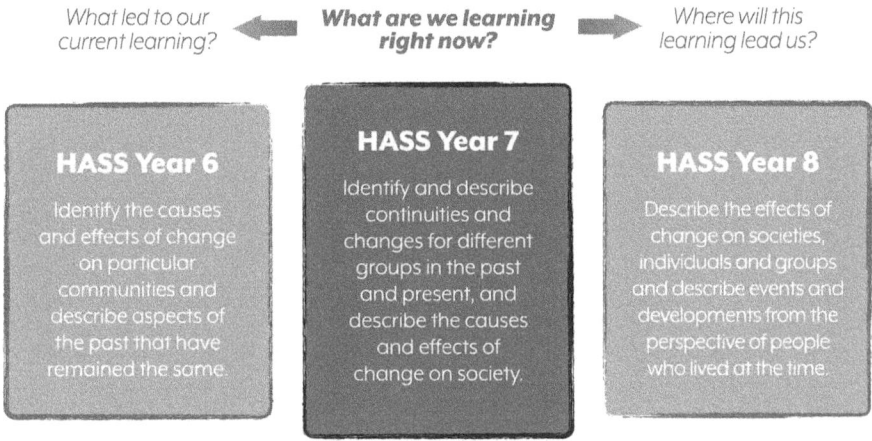

Figure 2.6: Identifying past and future learning between achievement standards in the Australian Curriculum.

Crafting learning intentions involves thinking about past and future learning. We ask, 'What was the learning that led to what we are learning now, and what learning will it lead to?' This is how knowledge and understanding connect within the curriculum. When we recognise prior and future learning, it allows us to support learners with diverse needs by providing them with the opportunity to work across a broad range.

Our learners will come to us possessing knowledge, concepts, skills, attitudes and beliefs obtained from their prior learning, which will influence their thinking. We only increase the chance that they will better recall and utilise what we teach when we direct them to engage that prior knowledge to make meaningful connections to newer information (Wenk, 2017).

How to Unpack Learning Intentions

Making the learning intentions clear for learners entails fostering comprehension of the parts of our speech. Therefore, we should begin the unpacking process by scrutinising the language of the learning intention and clarifying it with our learners. We can discern two main components within any learning intention when we observe closely: a well-framed learning intention includes both (1) a verb and (2) an object. The verb refers to actions associated with the intended cognitive process. The object, usually a noun, describes the knowledge learners must acquire and construct during the learning (see figure 2.7).

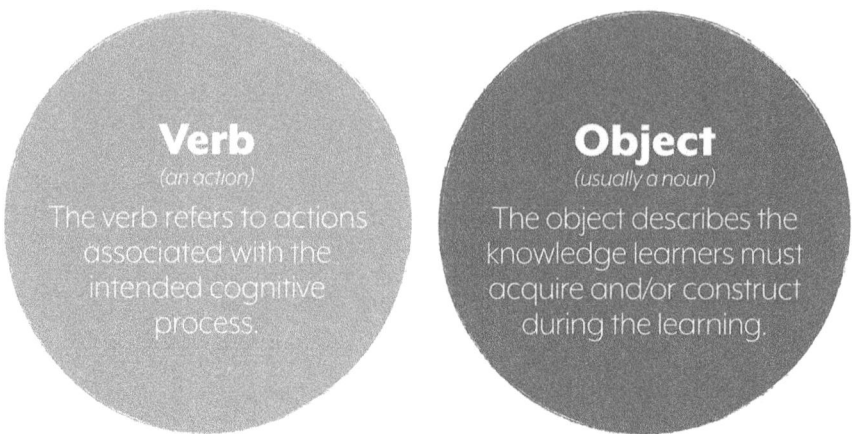

Figure 2.7: Verbs and objects, the two primary components of a learning intention.

The example in figure 2.8 demonstrates how you can simply identify verbs and objects in the learning intention by underlining the verbs and circling the objects. As you begin to unpack a learning intention with learners, you will discover a fantastic opportunity for cultivating literacy. You simply take the language already there and break out both the grammatical constructs and the actual words with your learners, subsequently providing literacy instruction in a practical way.

Figure 2.8: Unpacking learning intentions by underlining the verbs and circling the objects.

We can then create two categories of questions to clarify the learning intention and perform an in-depth examination of the objects and verbs: (1) unpacking questions and (2) purposeful questions. Formulating and exploring these questions presents an effective analytical and critical thinking exercise, as considering questions leads to exceptional thinking and the answers give rise to further questions and deeper inquiry.

Unpacking Questions

Unpacking questions focus on making the learning intentions clear by investigating the language of the learning – in this case, the verbs and objects we identified earlier. The fifth question in the following list of example unpacking questions demonstrates just how expansive these questions can become. By asking 'What does *significance* mean?' we are faced instantly with more and more specific lines of questioning. How do we decide what is significant? Who is responsible for making that decision? Who or what is this significant to? When something is significant to one person or group but insignificant to another, what are the implications? These increasingly distinct and ponderous considerations we generate are how we help our learners develop powerful and versatile analytical questioning skills for learning and life (Crockett, 2019).

Examples of unpacking questions include:

1. What does it mean to describe something?
2. What is it we will be describing?
3. What does it mean to explain something?
4. What will we be explaining?
5. What does *significance* mean?
6. What do you think *the development of Australia* means?
7. Are some events, people, groups, places, and events more significant than others to the development of Australia? Why?
8. Do you think any people, groups, places or events are insignificant? What would this mean for those groups?

Purposeful Questions

Purposeful questions, discussed in more detail in Chapter 3 (page 49), are meant to engage, lead and steer learners towards more and more possibilities, as well as create the opportunity to connect to multiple curricular outcomes. If we are diligent about our questioning, we can easily access various curricular areas as the focus of instruction. An example of this is the potential for curricular expansion that can be found in the first question of the following list of purposeful questions: 'If there were one thing you would want people to understand about Australia, what would it be?' Consider what this question could reveal concerning topics such as history, language, politics, geography, science, cultural studies and more.

Examples of purposeful questions include:

1. If there were one thing you would want people to understand about Australia, what would it be?
2. How have experiences of democracy and citizenship differed between groups over time and place?
3. How have key figures, events and values shaped Australian society, its system of government and citizenship?
4. How has Australia developed as a society with global connections, and what is my role as a global citizen?
5. Is Australia still developing?

Effectively unpacking learning intentions with your students involves identifying the verbs and objects in a learning intention and then asking these types of questions around them. Such questions help us uncover the expectations we have for learners in their learning and also show learners the directions the learning can go. In my work with schools, I consistently see significant improvements in literacy just from effectively unpacking learning intentions and not using other literacy interventions. For example, according to national norms, Lalor Primary School in Melbourne, Victoria, saw significantly higher levels of growth than expected in the ACER tests for reading and mathematics. Principal Trevor Robinson noted that this happened during the COVID-19 remote learning lockdown, which makes this outcome even more impressive.

Another important benefit of collectively unpacking learning intentions is that most of the learning happens *during* that process. Just going through the unpacking activity places your learners ahead of the game. We find that most of the schools we work with that explore learning intentions in this way reach a point where their learners are operating at three or four National Assessment Program – Literacy and Numeracy (NAPLAN) levels above where they are usually expected to be for literacy.

The key thing to understand is that asking purposeful questions around unpacking learning intentions is about *engaging* learners and leading them towards more possibilities. When looking at a learning intention, we must realise it's not confined to a particular activity or learning area and connects to many other things. Any learning intention should be broad enough to pose no limitations for learners on their opportunities for varied learning experiences (National Council for Curriculum and Assessment, 2015). Ultimately, conversations like these aim to clarify the intention, not to challenge learners to be correct. Learning is about engaging in discourse and discussion, which creates clarity. Taking the time to unpack learning intentions is about getting to know our learners and giving them a safe place to cultivate curiosity, foster agency and build higher-order thinking skills through wondering, imagining, critical reflection and evaluation. By extension, this makes it an ideal diagnostic assessment tool.

Diagnostic assessment is used to identify the strengths and weaknesses in a student's understanding and to subsequently allow the teacher to use this data to help in the effective planning of a lesson's trajectory. It is most often implemented at the commencement of the learning process, whether at the start of a unit to diagnose prior knowledge or at the beginning of a lesson to appraise a learner's internalisation and synthesis of a previous lesson's content (Crockett & Churches, 2017). Similarly, unpacking learning intentions also happens at the beginning of the learning process and serves the same diagnostic purpose. Through the unpacking process, learners explore their current knowledge and assumptions about the learning intention, which helps the teacher to pinpoint where the learners are in relation to the intentions they are discovering together.

Summary and Key Points

- To become successful with agency, it is essential that learners understand what they are learning, why they are learning and how they will know they are successful.

- Learning intentions are the what, why and how of learning, and the success criteria represent the goals learners must strive to reach.

- Learning intentions are about essential understandings, critical concepts and individual perspectives.

- Learning intentions are about *what we are learning*, and lesson objectives are about *what we are doing*.

- Exploring a learning intention effectively spans a more extended period than simply an individual lesson.

- With any learning intention, we should be able to identify previous and future learning intentions, all of which are linked together.

- Unpacking a learning intention begins with clarifying the language by identifying the object and verb and then forming two types of questions around the learning intention, *unpacking questions* and *purposeful questions*.

Guiding Questions

1. What is the purpose of learning intentions and success criteria, and what do they tell us?
2. What are the three concepts that define what a learning intention is, and why are they important?
3. How does the clarification of learning intentions and success criteria foster learner agency?
4. What is the fundamental difference between a learning intention and a lesson objective, and why is this important?
5. How is learning connected between the past, present and future?

6. Why should we unpack learning intentions with our learners, and what is the simplest and most effective way to begin this process?

7. Why do we ask purposeful questions when unpacking learning intentions with learners?

Chapter 3

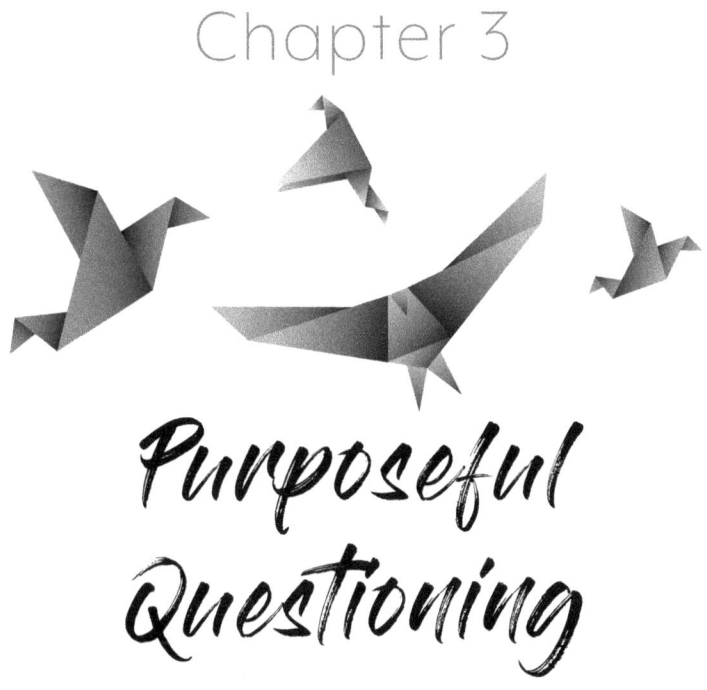

Purposeful Questioning

It is not the answer that enlightens, but the question.
Eugene Ionesco, *78 Important Questions Every Leader Should Ask and Answer*

Asking purposeful questions is a cornerstone of learning and living, and it is a practice we use every day. If you think about it, the majority of our success in life depends on asking the best questions and making the best decisions. I believe that the vast majority of our learners' formative experiences in school should be focused on advancing their capacity for agency so they can learn to ask the best questions and make the best decisions for a lifetime. The transition from teachers' agents to learner agency is reflected in the transition from *telling* to *asking*. As educators, there is no denying that what we ask our learners is critical, but even more critical is *how* we ask it.

All learning begins with questions, and how we model questioning for our learners will define the quality of their learning (Crockett, 2019). Without meaningful questions and learning in context, the purpose of learning is lost. Asking purposeful questions gives our learners permission to be curious and creative, and strive for more profound knowledge and meaningful answers.

The mechanics of a teacher's questioning technique should be diverse and include a range of questions with different purposes if they wish to promote a high level of critical thinking capacity and agency with learning (Carpenter & Pease, 2013). The problem is that we do not focus enough on the kind of questioning behaviours that allow learners to take agency over what we are teaching so that teachers can move from posing the majority of the questions to asking only guiding questions here and there while the learners create their own questions through inquiry and critical thinking.

Research indicates that even though the average teacher spends roughly 40 per cent of class time asking questions, ineffective practices such as asking primarily lower-cognitive-level questions, focusing more questions on a limited number of students, giving learners little or no time to respond effectively and crafting questions in a linear direction that favours control over stimulating free thinking are still the norm in classrooms (Arslan, 2006). The same study suggests that 'a teacher's questioning technique, correlating with enhanced achievement, should include a balance of convergent and divergent questions, probing questions, listening to student responses, redirecting student responses to other students, providing respectful feedback and allowing for appropriate time after asking a question' (Arslan, 2006, p. 82).

Another study (Almeida, 2012) asserts, 'it is well-known that teachers typically ask low-level questions, whose answers require mainly memory', and that 'the findings on teachers' characteristic use of low-cognitive-level questions have been verified at all school levels, from elementary teaching to university' (p. 2). It seems then that the pursuit of purposeful questioning is often ignored as a proactive enhancement of the teaching and learning process. Yet other researchers argue that 'the nature and intention of the questions used in instructional settings, as well as the use of strategies used by the teacher in asking and eliciting responses to create meaningful dialogue in the classrooms, are central to an effective learning environment' (Crowe & Stanford, 2010, p. 36). This chapter will help educators craft purposeful questions to both engage an audience of learners and elicit discussion on increasingly specific content areas as required by the curriculum.

Why Purposeful Questioning Matters

One of the 10 Shifts of Practice I identified in *Future-Focused Learning* is essential and herding questions (Crockett, 2019). I mentioned specifically that asking significant questions leads to broad exceptional thinking, and answers lead to more questions and more in-depth inquiry. We explore possibility and potential in ourselves and the world around us using such questions. I illustrate this through the following exemplar from *Future-Focused Learning*:

> For example, perhaps the curriculum you want to address involves medicine and diseases. An essential question you might ask students is, 'How best can we ensure everyone's health?' In reply, students may talk about obesity, nutrition or healthy eating. They may discuss exercise, safe streets or wearing a bicycle helmet. It doesn't matter which direction the conversation takes, as long as they all engage in dialogue and debate. Even though they are a long way from where you intended (medicine and diseases), you can use their ideas and the engagement you established to ask a series of herding questions such as, 'If all that works, and you're living a healthy lifestyle and wearing a bike helmet, what happens if you suddenly become ill? What happens if you get a disease? Do you know anyone who has ever had a terminal illness?' (Crockett, 2019, p. 10)

Valuing the quality of questions rather than simply emphasising the need for correct responses drives higher levels of thinking (Almeida, 2012). For example, would philosophy exist if we had not asked, 'What is real? Is there a meaning to life? If so, what is it?' Consider the multitude of questions and disciplines that have arisen from that curiosity over centuries. How much more understanding of ourselves and our world do we have now because someone dared to be curious long ago? This is why I believe that purposeful, essential questions are essential to meaningful learning and the development of learner agency.

How to Make Questions Essential

An *essential question* is a guiding question used to introduce learning or as the basis of an inquiry. It may be that it is at the beginning of a lengthy unit of work or that it is a provocation for a single concept used in only one lesson. An essential question is also a question that leads us to explore the background of a problem and choose from various plans, strategies or possible courses of action to generate a complex, applicable solution. The point is that it is essential to the learning (see figure 3.1).

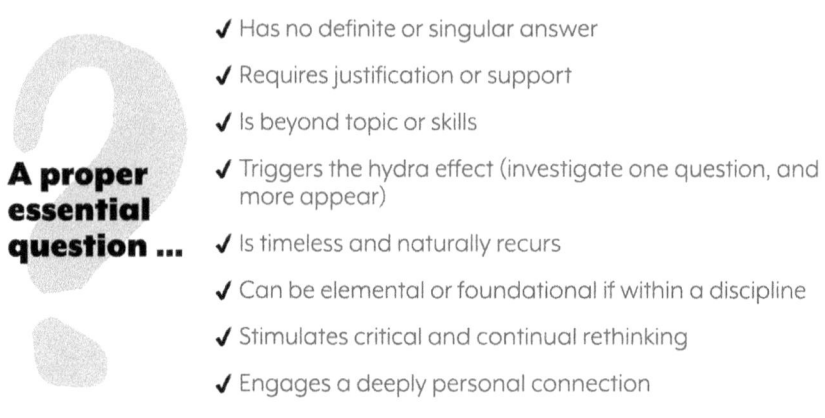

Figure 3.1: The characteristics of a proper essential question.

The following sections detail two approaches to making questions essential:

1. the two-step approach
2. essential understandings and essential questions.

The Two-Step Approach

In my work with teachers, I generally lead conversations about essential questions by progressively crossing out the nonessential parts of a question and then rewriting them underneath. As I progressed with this method in session after session, I noticed a distinct pattern of thought emerging that revealed what I consider today to be one of the simplest methods for consistently engineering purposeful essential questions. It is an approach that consists of only two steps:

1. **Move the question higher on Bloom's revised taxonomy.** Figure 3.2 illustrates the six levels of thinking skills according to Bloom's revised taxonomy (Anderson & Krathwohl, 2001), with lower-level cognitive skills at the bottom of the figure and higher-level skills at the top. Use this chart to transform your question

from simple recall (or remembering, the lowest level on the chart) to a question involving in-depth analysis, evaluation or creation (higher-order thinking skills on Bloom's revised taxonomy). Moving your questions higher on Bloom's revised taxonomy naturally increases engagement and relevance. The definitions of the stages of the taxonomy in figure 3.2 show how your question improves as it moves up the taxonomy.

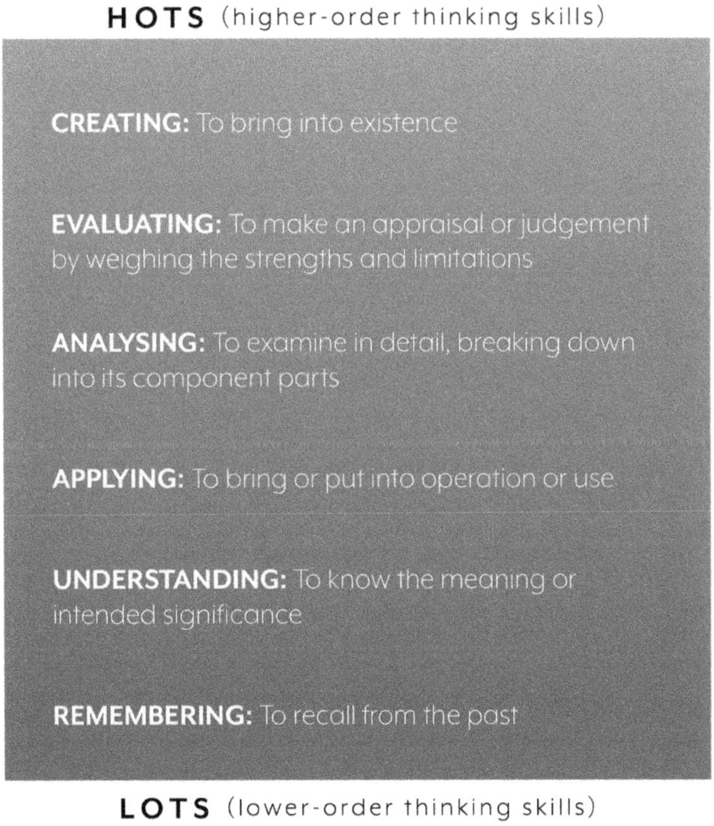

HOTS (higher-order thinking skills)

CREATING: To bring into existence

EVALUATING: To make an appraisal or judgement by weighing the strengths and limitations

ANALYSING: To examine in detail, breaking down into its component parts

APPLYING: To bring or put into operation or use

UNDERSTANDING: To know the meaning or intended significance

REMEMBERING: To recall from the past

LOTS (lower-order thinking skills)

Source: Adapted from Anderson & Krathwohl, 2001.

Figure 3.2: The levels of Bloom's revised taxonomy.

2. **Remove specificity.** This technique is about removing focus. Figure 3.3 (page 54) provides an example of a simple, not particularly engaging nonessential question driven by the content a teacher might want a class to learn ('What native plants do we use in our daily lives?'). By removing concepts from the

question and broadening its focus, we can ask questions with increasing relevance – and of greater interest – to a wider range of learners. The broad question is the essential question; the increasingly specific questions that arise from this then become your herding questions that drive learners into more profound discovery and learning. We will discuss herding questions in more detail in the section on 'Learner Wrangling and Herding Questions' (page 57).

What indigenous plants do we use in our daily lives?

▼

How do the ~~indigenous plants~~ **we use in our** ~~daily lives~~ **affect us?**

▼

How do living things affect ~~us?~~

▼

How do we ~~and living things~~ **affect each other?**

▼

How do we affect each other?

Figure 3.3: Removing specificity from nonessential questions to broaden their focus and create an essential question.

The following is an example of the two-step approach in action. We begin with a specific question, move it up Bloom's revised taxonomy and then gradually remove specificity.

Who was Julius Caesar?

This is not a great question for many reasons. It is easily answered with a quick internet search, offers no opportunity for deeper investigative learning and is highly specific and final. Now observe what happens when we begin to work with the two steps.

Was Julius Caesar or Marcus Aurelius a better ruler?

This question requires evaluation, which puts it near the top of Bloom's taxonomy. But it is simple to create a response that likely would not engage or inspire debate. Now we will remove the specificity of the two historical figures and see what happens.

What qualities should a great leader have?

At this point, the evaluation is much deeper, causing the learner to develop a set of criteria based on personal judgment and views. We can, however, remove the specificity of the historical role and choose a broader concept, as shown by the next question.

What makes a great leader?

This question still requires an evaluation and the development of criteria, but it now inspires more inquiry as more questions arise. But while this question is excellent, we can give it an even more significant boost with fewer specifics and a higher place on Bloom's revised taxonomy.

What is greatness?

This is a truly essential question, and each previous question is a more specific subset. With greatness, we consider great leaders, devotion, sacrifice and humility. With leadership, a subgroup could be heads of state and, ultimately, a particular individual. Depending on the interests of your class, your discussion could go in several different directions while still having relevance to the overall learning.

Essential Understandings and Essential Questions

There is an even more straightforward way to create an essential question, and it requires only one step. According to *Understanding by Design* by Grant Wiggins and Jay McTighe (2005), an essential question calls for higher-order thinking tasks such as analysis, inference, evaluation and prediction. It cannot be effectively answered by recall alone and points towards important transferable ideas within (and sometimes across) disciplines. Wiggins and McTighe (2005) remind us that essential questions are 'questions that are not answerable with finality in a brief sentence … their aim is to stimulate thought, to provoke inquiry, and to spark more questions – including thoughtful student questions – not just pat answers' (p. 106).

We will look now at a few examples of essential questions:

How do the arts shape as well as reflect a culture?

Is there ever a 'just' war?

Is any history capable of escaping the social and personal history of its writers?

How does where you live influence how you live?

Ask yourself, what do I feel might be the essential understandings there? What elements of the curriculum are points I would want to have appear for learners? How might that shape my learners' thinking?

The point I want to make clear here is this: an essential question is just an essential understanding with a question mark. When learners have the agency to critically reflect on questions like the ones mentioned previously, they begin to consider what matters to them, what they believe and what they disagree with. It helps them to form actual personalities. Research confirms that 'students' questions play an important role in meaningful learning and motivation, and can be very revealing about the quality of students' thinking and conceptual understanding, their alternative frameworks and confusion about various concepts, their reasoning, and what they want to know' (Almeida, 2012, p. 2).

The essential understandings are the intention behind the learning and the more profound things that are meant to come. They define what it means to be educated, which is a conversation we don't have enough. Essential understandings enable learners to determine whom they will become by reflecting on the opinions, beliefs and attitudes they have about these essential understandings.

An essential question is just an essential understanding with a question mark.

Recall the example learning intention from the Australian Curriculum we introduced in figure 2.4 (page 37): 'Describe and explain the significance of people, groups, places, and events to the development of Australia.' From this learning intention we can draw three essential understandings, as shown in figure 3.4. Having identified these essential understandings, it is a simple one-step task to transform them into essential questions by rephrasing the statement in the form of a question.

Purposeful Questioning

Figure 3.4: Transforming essential understandings into essential questions.

Essential questions are intended to provoke movement. They are broad and complex as they are are meant to stimulate thinking and engage as many learners as possible. Once there is movement, how do you guide the class discussion from those questions to what they need to learn? The answer is through herding questions.

Learner Wrangling and Herding Questions

Meaningful answers require more than one or two questions. As educators, when we ask one question and get one response, we have missed many opportunities to go exponentially deeper, driving towards essential understandings. The best way to illustrate this is by using our previously mentioned examples. These are deep and powerful questions, and perhaps a bit overwhelming for learners right out of the gate. If we presented these to learners and left them alone, they would likely have no idea where to go with them. They are not yet involved with the questions to the degree they could be, and we have to help them along. We do that through the use of herding questions, which are designed to move learners by engaging, leading or steering them towards an outcome.

There are three types of herding questions, as shown in figure 3.5.

Engaging Questions
uncover the learner's personal connection, story, or voice. They initiate the momentum essential to activate the learning.

Leading Questions
identify and clarify the line of inquiry, and draw the learners toward it and toward the desired outcomes.

Steering Questions
guide learners to the line of inquiry and align the learners, and propel them to the desired outcomes.

Figure 3.5: The three types of herding questions: engaging questions, leading questions and steering questions.

Referring back to our three examples of essential questions in figure 3.4 (page 57), we begin to explore possibilities for herding questions.

Engaging Questions

Beginning with engaging questions, we look for specific connections learners have regarding the essential questions that get them moving in an exploratory direction:

1. What makes Australia special to you?
2. Is your story only an Australian story, or are there other countries in your story?
3. How does it feel to be an Australian?
4. How does it feel to belong?
5. Does everyone feel the same? Why?
6. What are the important places in your life?
7. Do you feel you belong to the place where you live?

It is easy to see how rich and revealing the conversations between youself and learners could get with this line of questioning. In the past, some teachers have expressed to me their concerns about inquiry taking learners 'all over the place', but this is a good thing. Your learners are unique individuals with varying perspectives and ideas. By using engaging questions, you are already initiating the momentum essential to activate learning (see figure 3.6).

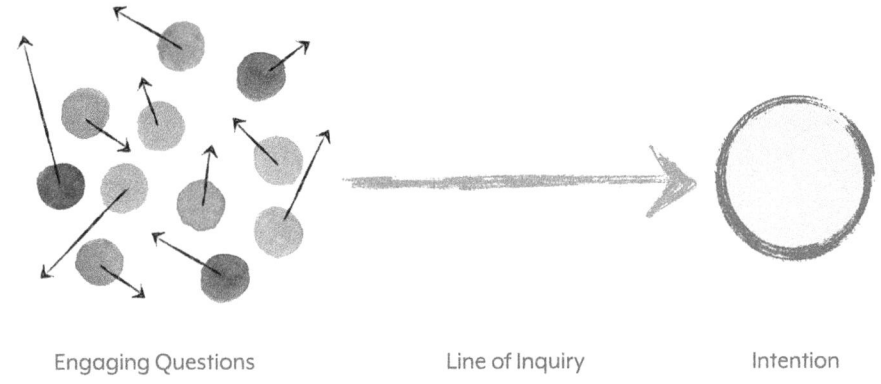

Source: © 2022 by Lee Crockett, Future-Focused Learning Network, Purposeful Questioning masterclass.
Figure 3.6: Using engaging questions to explore learners' personal connections to learning.

If you recall high school physics class, you learned about momentum. Momentum is simply the force or energy gained by a moving object. This describes linear or angular momentum effectively enough, but it also addresses a critical concept for us to consider: for there to be momentum, there must be forward motion. Achieving momentum can be said to be the primary purpose of engaging questions. We are only using provocations for our learners, seeking to gain movement and engagement. Once learners are engaged in answering questions and begin to move in any direction, we can introduce the next portion of herding questions – the leading questions – from which we build on the learners' momentum and draw them towards the line of inquiry.

Leading Questions

The following are examples of leading questions:

1. When does Australia's story begin?
2. How do we hear, learn or remember the stories of the past?

3. Do you feel that Australia's whole story has been heard?
4. If you were Australia's voice, what would you say? Are you Australia's voice?
5. Who is the voice of Australia? Is there only one voice?
6. Does Australia have a story? Does Australia have more than one story?
7. Do places have different meanings for different people?

These questions are designed to lead the learners towards the line of inquiry. We've taken them from going in multiple directions and begun drawing them towards the line of inquiry and the desired outcome (see figure 3.7).

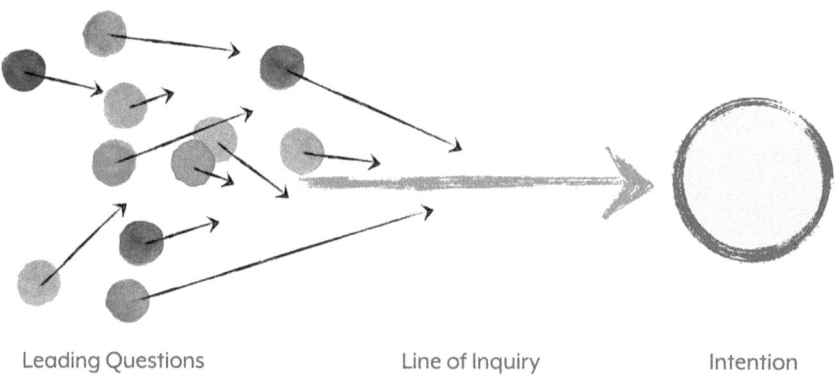

Leading Questions   Line of Inquiry   Intention

Source: © 2022 by Lee Crockett, Future-Focused Learning Network, Purposeful Questioning masterclass.

Figure 3.7: Leading questions draw learners towards the line of inquiry.

Up to this point, we have employed engaging questions to get learners moving and we have used leading questions to draw them to the line of inquiry, but we are still leading the discussion at this point. This is very much an example of guided inquiry and remains heavily teacher-centred in many ways. The last set of questions – steering questions – is when we truly take our hands off the inquiry wheel and allow learners to take agency for their learning.

Steering Questions

At this stage, we ask the types of questions that encourage learners to break down complex ideas into more manageable concepts help them to visualise relationships between these concepts and to generalise the learning as inquiry becomes deeper (Crowe & Stanford, 2010). Our questions become more attuned to higher-level thinking skills such as problem-solving, analysis and knowledge creation, which are preferable for this stage because, as one study points out, 'a student needs to have a deep understanding of the topic in order to answer his type of question' (Arslan, 2006, p. 84).

The following are examples of steering questions:

1. What happens to the story or the history if not every perspective is included?
2. How does this story, history or version compare to that one?
3. How can we ensure that everyone is included?
4. Who is responsible for making everyone feel included?
5. How is your voice, story or perspective heard? How do you know?
6. How might you best share your story?
7. Is there another perspective we need to include?
8. Is one voice, story or perspective more important than another? Why?
9. What is a Welcome to Country?
10. Who is responsible for this?

These new questions are now steering learners along the line of inquiry. What we are doing is taking the learners and pushing them from behind (see figure 3.8, page 62). We are no longer leading them; some are out front leading themselves while others will follow, and other questions or conversations will happen.

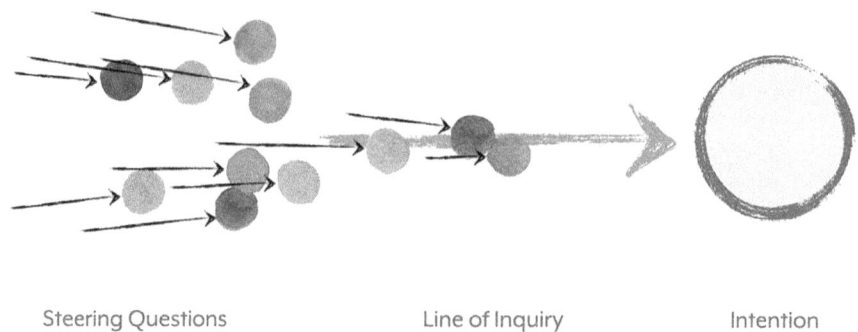

Steering Questions   Line of Inquiry   Intention

Source: © 2022 by Lee Crockett, Future-Focused Learning Network, Purposeful Questioning masterclass.
Figure 3.8: Steering questions allow learners to begin practising true agency over learning.

At this point we no longer need to run the discussion. We can step back and apply pressure where needed to continue to move things forward. Steering questions align learners towards the line of inquiry, propelling them towards the desired outcomes.

Now, if we think back to the essential question, did we answer the essential question? Not really. What we have accomplished instead is a cultivation of the essential understandings, which is the fundamental purpose of inquiry. Our goal is not to answer or to solve the essential question but rather to gain a deeper appreciation and understanding of it. That is why our essential questions can afford to be so expansive and why they can have more than one answer. It is through the implementation of the three types of herding questions – engaging, leading and steering questions – that we will propel learners to where we need them to go while simultaneously guiding them to foster agency for their learning. This is how we move from telling to asking.

Summary and Key Points

- The transition from teacher agents to learner agency is reflected in the transition from *telling* to *asking*.

- Learning begins with asking questions, and how we model questioning for learners defines the quality of their learning.

- Creating essential questions should be our goal as educators – consistently asking learners questions that are timeless and open, and that lead to thoughtful discussion and even more questions.

- You can make a question more essential simply by moving it up Bloom's revised taxonomy and removing specificity.

- An essential question is just an essential understanding with a question mark.

- There are three types of questions we use to engage our learners meaningfully, build agency and critical thinking skills and move them towards a line of inquiry.

Guiding Questions

1. Why do we question?
2. Why is how we ask just as important as, if not more important, what we ask?
3. What is a truly *essential* question?
4. What are essential questions meant to do in learning?
5. What happens when we give the learners the agency to reflect critically on the questions we ask?
6. In the beginning stages of inquiry, why give learners the freedom to go in different directions with their thinking?
7. What is the result of learners fostering agency through purposeful questioning, and how does this transform the role of a teacher?

Chapter 4

Lesson Zero

Start where you are. Use what you have. Do what you can.

Arthur Ashe, *Days of Grace: A Memoir*

Recall the Chapter 2 discussion on learning intentions and lesson objectives and how they differ. The takeaway was to be aware that what learners are doing in a lesson is not what they are learning. Learning intentions are essentially the achievement standards, and they are both the beginning point and the destination, measurable by success criteria. Our (lesson) objectives are the steps we are taking to arrive there. We also know that learning intentions are about what learners are learning, why they are learning and how they will know they are successful, and that these are often confused with lesson objectives, which are the actual tasks being performed in the lesson. As a clarification for embarking on our exploration of our next concept, Lesson Zero, consider the following:

- learning intention = what we are learning
- purpose = why we are learning
- success criteria = how we will know we are successful
- lesson objectives = what we are doing to learn this.

It is essential to understand that if you do not actively communicate learning intentions, learners know nothing about the unit of learning. They are entirely in the dark, navigating the darkness alone, and there is no opportunity for them to exercise agency because they have no control or input and no notion of what will happen.

Say this is the case for your learners. Then suddenly, seemingly out of nowhere, a lesson arrives for them. Without prior knowledge or context, they have no idea what the lesson will be about or why it is being presented. They do their best to follow along and to try to figure out what, if anything, just happened. Finally the lesson ends and, if motivated, learners may then reflect on what it was all about. Then the next day, another lesson is presented in what becomes a seemingly endless stream. Occasionally a quiz or test gets thrown in to break the monotony. After a continuation of this cycle, learners begin to wonder how long this will go on, still without knowing why.

Is it any wonder that learners seem to struggle with taking the initiative when given the opportunity? Years of this do not empower them to be independent. It teaches them that their job is strictly to show up, that school is where children are forced to go to watch teachers work. There is no room for agency in this scenario and no options for moving at any other pace than that set by the teacher. This is the pedagogy of the oppressed, and the only options for a learner are passive submission or active subversion. In this structure learners are limited to and by the teaching itself.

> *This is the pedagogy of the oppressed, and the only options for a learner are passive submission or active subversion.*

Without any idea of a direction, purpose or destination, learners are wholly lost, which brings us back to the all-important question of why they are learning and how these lessons are connected. How do we ensure our learners benefit from clarity and simplicity with learning intentions and success criteria before embarking on a unit of learning? Enter Lesson Zero.

What is Lesson Zero?

Simply put, Lesson Zero is what happens before any of our other lessons begin. It is when we take the time to set up the unit of work and unpack the learning intentions and success criteria with the learners. The concept of

Lesson Zero originated from my many in-depth discussions with teachers about unpacking learning intentions. The question that constantly arose in our conversations was regarding time allocation. Educators often asked me if learning intentions should be unpacked over one or two lessons, and they wanted specifics. I always responded the same way, saying unpacking learning intentions should take as long as needed. As I mentioned in Chapter 2 (page 29), the unpacking process is something we cannot rush through if we genuinely want it to be effective for our learners.

It is understandable that, if you are new to the process of using purposeful questioning to facilitate learner agency, you might be nervous about the prospect of spending undefined time unpacking learning intentions with your students. After all, you likely have a finite time in which to teach each specific unit of content, so Lesson Zero can't be indefinite.

In response, firstly I would ask you to shift your thinking from 'I have a finite time in which to teach this' to something that is more accurate: 'My learners have a finite amount of time in which to learn this.' Learning, not teaching, is the outcome we are striving for, and unless we begin to think from this perspective, we will continue to believe that teaching content is necessary and is our responsibility. It is not. We are responsible for the learning, and with this new mindset, we can begin to explore how best to achieve that learning. Teaching is only one option through which it can be learned.

Additionally, I would ask you to recall our discussion about Hattie's (2008) effect sizes from Chapter 2 (page 40), in which we stated that an effect size of 1.0 is similar to the advancement of learners' achievement by one school year or a rate of improvement in learning by about 50 per cent, with learning intentions and success criteria having an effect size of 0.75 (Hattie, 2008). There are two points I wish to make regarding effect sizes. The first is that although Hattie indicates the apparent efficacy of learning intentions, his research does not indicate how to effectively employ them with learners, so without a quantifiable methodology, the effect size of your students might vary dramatically from that of another educator. The Agents to Agency Teacher and Learner Continuums you will find in Chapter 6 (page 101) demonstrate how wide this variance can be and will allow you to identify where your practice is now and the next steps to deepen your use of learning intentions.

The second is that Hattie (2008) mentions the effect size of using learning intentions is 0.75, which means that it accelerates learning by almost one school year. The question is, how much effect size is lost if we spend our initial time engaging in Lesson Zero before any actual learning begins? The answer is that the return on investment, or ROI, for our invested time is exponential, and we should not be concerned with how long it takes to do this properly. I will discuss an example from a school in Dubai later in the chapter, when we explore Lesson Zero in action.

Remember as well the study mentioned previously from the University of Glasgow (Crichton & Mcdaid, 2016). The researchers draw two conclusions that we can apply to Lesson Zero:

1. Learners want learning intentions and success criteria used thoroughly, with ample time devoted to their discussion and clarification.

2. The time you spend executing Lesson Zero comes back many times over and accelerates learning.

Rushing into learning without adequately preparing for the learning by thoroughly using Lesson Zero would be like running out the door without your pants on because you were too concerned with getting to work to prepare appropriately. It just would not make sense. Please keep the above two points in mind, because Lesson Zero takes as long as it takes, there is no point in moving forward otherwise, and it will pay dividends in time and outcomes. I am sure that both more time and better outcomes are vital to you.

Lesson Zero in Action

For many years I have had the privilege of working with GEMS Education in Dubai. Written above the entrance way to one of their schools is a quote from the chairman, Sunny Varkey: 'Whatever the question, education is the answer.' I think we can all agree with this statement, and I have often turned it around by asking teachers, 'If the learning you are providing is the answer, what was the question?' How can we just begin learning without establishing the need? The answer, of course, is that we cannot. Lesson Zero is, as mentioned previously, 'navigating the darkness'.

Lesson Zero comprises four parts, to be discussed in the following sections:

1. provocation
2. learning intentions
3. success criteria
4. determination of first steps.

1. Provocation

As I emphasise in *Future-Focused Learning*, 'To learn something, it must stimulate your curiosity – in other words, interest precedes learning' (Crockett, 2019, p. 21). Lesson Zero begins with provocation, which can take many forms. A common and powerful provocation is the use of an essential question, the construction and use of which we thoroughly discussed in the preceding chapter (page 49). Provocation can also be physical, as is often employed in play-based learning, such as through providing objects to explore and understand. It can also be experiential.

I remember a high school class where the teacher presented a manufactured news article showing China had outright purchased Australia due to the national debt. The report listed all the rights and freedoms that would be revoked immediately. There was an uproar from the learners, who were not shy in voicing their concerns. After a while, the teacher revealed the article was fake and asked the learners to reflect on how it feels when some external body forces itself on them. This was used as a provocation to introduce the learning around the colonisation and federation of Australia, a topic that is often challenging for learners to relate to. It was remarked that the engagement and outcomes within the class were notably improved compared with classes in previous years. The import of provocation is that it fosters curiosity and intrigue, establishing a need for and the intention of the learning.

2. Learning Intentions

With interest and purpose firmly established, we present the learning intentions, making them clear for the learners by thoroughly unpacking the intentions and asking purposeful questions as detailed in the previous chapter (page 49). When we successfully unpack learning intentions with our learners, we automatically establish the purpose for them. They create a personal connection to the learning deepening the purpose we established through provocation.

3. Success Criteria

The value of co-constructing success criteria with learners is often not appreciated. If we just provide success criteria, we remove the opportunity for agency. Additionally, providing or explaining the learning intention and success criteria and simply asking if there are any questions does not ensure an understanding of either. Only when learners are able to effectively construct success criteria are we certain they understand the learning intention. More importantly, they are exercising agency. Through building the success criteria themselves, they accept both the challenge and the responsibility for the outcome.

In my experience, this crucial step is the most often overlooked or avoided. When it comes to success criteria and outcomes, it is challenging for us to let go of control. I would suggest we are not letting go of control, only the illusion of control. I recommend the first few times to construct success criteria beforehand so you are clear on what success looks like and what you are prepared to accept. Then, when facilitating the co-construction, lead your learners to arrive at the same point. Usually, after having done this a few times, teachers are quite comfortable doing this in real time.

Interestingly, once we have established the success criteria, we no longer need to consider the learning intention. We use it to build the success criteria, which is our endpoint. Once we have done that and the learning intention remains visible, we can focus on the destination.

In my masterclasses and work with schools, I recommend constructing success criteria against the levels of Bloom's revised taxonomy, which I find to be the most effective and helpful resource for this purpose. Organising and constructing success criteria against taxonomic levels accomplishes several things. Firstly, it provides a variety of choices for learners, all of which evidence the learning intention. This allows for personalisation and fosters agency. Additionally, it provides differentiation for a diverse range of learners and capabilities. Further, it means that a group of learners will produce a variety of responses to the learning, which provides a significant opportunity for learners to reflect on the depth of the learning intention as they self- and peer-assess. It further reinforces that in school, just as in life, there is rarely one correct answer.

The book *Mindful Assessment* relied on Bloom's revised taxonomy to construct rubrics for the most complicated outcomes (Crockett & Churches, 2017). The process of building a range of success criteria is significantly more straightforward. On page 53 we formed an understanding of the taxonomic levels we will use to construct success criteria.

Think back to Chapter 2, when we discussed unpacking learning intentions (page 42) and worked with an example of the Australian Curriculum. The example was as follows:

> *Describes and explains the significance of people, groups, places and events to the development of Australia.*

If you were to co-construct success criteria with your learners against the various levels of Bloom's revised taxonomy, they might look something like what is illustrated in table 4.1 (page 72).

The examples in table 4.1 are merely a sampling of any number of possibilities, depending on your learners' specific talents, interests and concerns. Here is the good news: you can create criteria such as these very quickly, with no need to spend days on end going through them with learners. Once you place the unpacked learning intention in front of them and start using Bloom's revised taxonomy to co-construct success criteria, it will amaze you how quickly they pick it up. Figure 4.1 (page 73) is an example of success criteria developed by Year 4 learners at Lalor Primary School, based on the learning intention 'Understand what fractions represent and link by investigating strategies to solve problems involving adding and subtracting fractions'.

Table 4.1: Constructing success criteria using Bloom's revised taxonomy.

CREATING	Create an historical narrative that tells the story of the significance of an event or development, individual or group from a particular perspective. What is the version of this time in history that you believe should be told?
EVALUATING	Compare experiences of Australian democracy and citizenship in the 1900s, including the status and rights of Aboriginal and Torres Strait Islander peoples, migrants, women and children, to identify different perspectives and communicate your own point of view.
ANALYSING	Choose a technological innovation and analyse its function in Australian society, past or present. For example, the aerodynamics of traditional tools such as boomerangs or spears, or the first Australian-built aircraft in 1910.
APPLYING	Develop a set of questions you would want to ask someone from a time in history if you could go back and interview them. As a historian reporting back to our time, what would you want to know?
UNDERSTANDING	Explain the significance of a traditional story shared by First Nations custodians of the land you live on. What does this story teach you about the land on which you live?
REMEMBERING	Construct a timeline of significant events 1900–2020, considering a particular issue or theme in Australian society. Create a map identifying the traditional lands or language groups of First Nations peoples.

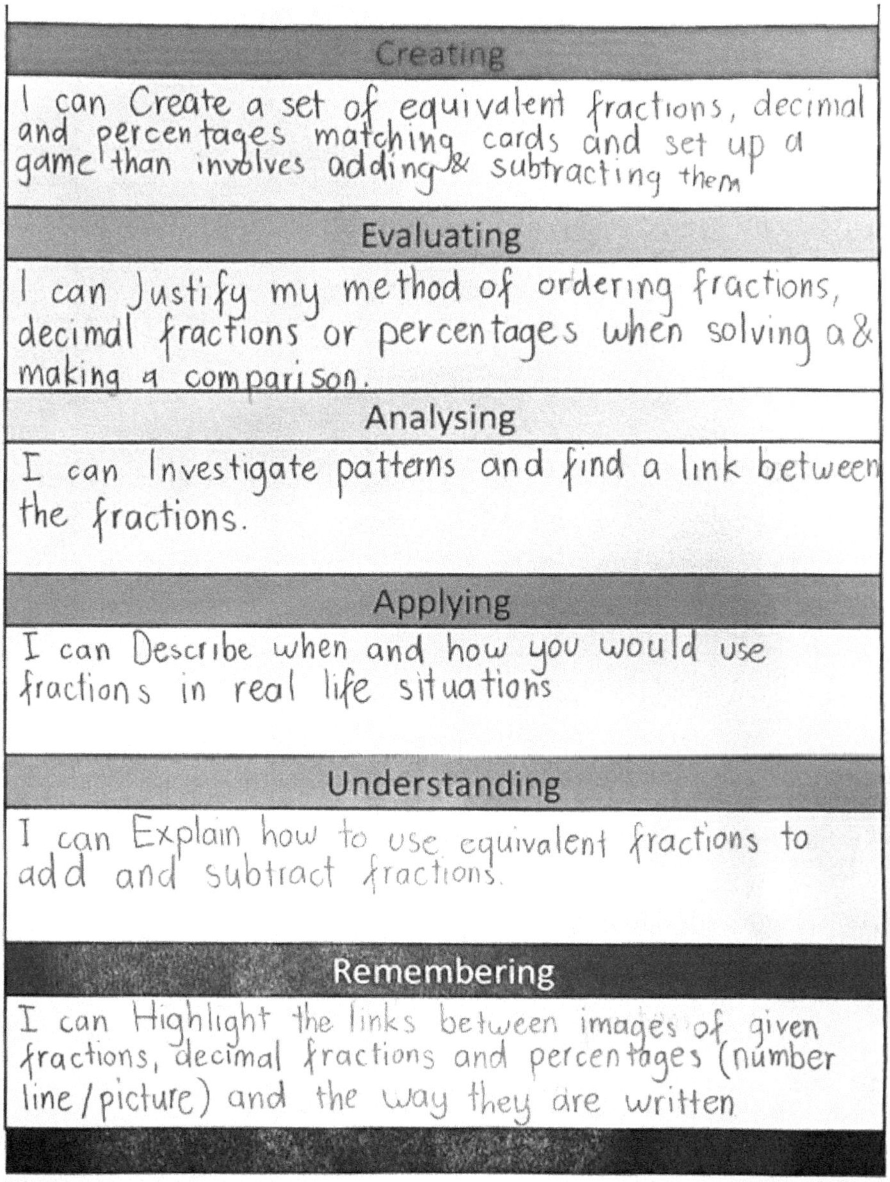

Creating
I can Create a set of equivalent fractions, decimal and percentages matching cards and set up a game than involves adding & subtracting them
Evaluating
I can Justify my method of ordering fractions, decimal fractions or percentages when solving a & making a comparison.
Analysing
I can Investigate patterns and find a link between the fractions.
Applying
I can Describe when and how you would use fractions in real life situations
Understanding
I can Explain how to use equivalent fractions to add and subtract fractions.
Remembering
I can Highlight the links between images of given fractions, decimal fractions and percentages (number line/picture) and the way they are written

Source: © 2022 by Lalor Primary School. Used with permission.

Figure 4.1: Success criteria developed by Year 4 learners at Lalor Primary School.

As a note of caution, I have found during masterclasses and workshops that a few levels are so often confused that I would like to take a moment to make them clear. The misunderstanding is due to our use of language.

For example, take the word *evaluate*, as presented in the revised taxonomy. This term is often used when another might be preferable. For example, in mathematics, if *evaluate* means to make an appraisal or judgment (see figure 3.2, page 53), then we do not evaluate an *equation*, we *solve* an equation. Making this distinction in command terms, as discussed in *Mindful Assessment*, clarifies our intention for learners (Crockett & Churches, 2017).

The other area of confusion is our use of the word *create*. Often I will see success criteria for the create level written as something like, 'Create a graph that demonstrates your results.' This criterion is actually not at the create level but rather at the application level, and should be worded as, 'Construct a graph that demonstrates your results.' An example properly reflecting the create level might be, 'Create a unique method to demonstrate your results.' *Apply* and *create* are both external outputs, whereas the other levels are internal processes, and as such, they are often confused.

I know this from experience – no matter what school or even year level I am working with – every time I have presented learners with this approach, beginning with a simple understanding of Bloom's as in the one in figure 3.2 (page 53), they can construct success criteria themselves before I know it. More importantly, as mentioned previously, learners are not focused solely on one correct answer but instead embrace a range of possibilities.

4. Determination of First Steps

Now that we have established our learning intentions and success criteria, it is time to begin letting the learners take control. They reflect on the established intention for learning and the success criteria, determine which criteria they have already met and choose the first steps in the learning process, which you can negotiate and mutually determine (see figure 4.2). This is where learner agency begins, by giving learners a structure in which they can succeed. It is also, as we mentioned in Chapter 2, a diagnostic assessment strategy.

Lesson Zero

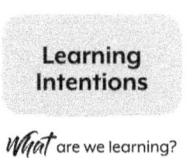  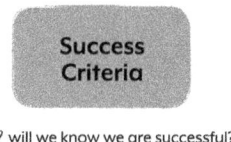

1. **Provocation** to foster curiosity and intrigue
2. **Unpack** the **Learning Intentions** and establish **Purpose**
3. **Co-construct** the **Success Criteria** [*You do this before and lead learners to arrive at the same point*]
4. **Learners reflect** on what **Success Criteria** they have already met and determine the first steps

Source: © 2022 by Lee Crockett, Future-Focused Learning Network, Learning Intentions 2.0 masterclass.
Figure 4.2: The Lesson Zero pathway.

Lesson Zero Case Study

Let us now take a closer look at how Lesson Zero might play out by once again using our curriculum exemplar from Chapter 2. This curricular standard can be adapted by changing the country's name, and it will still work perfectly as an example.

> *Describes and explains the significance of people, groups, places and events to the development of Australia.*

In the past, when I have presented this to teachers as an example, they sometimes feel the need to get stuck in certain historical periods or to focus on specific individuals and generally limit themselves in terms of what they choose to explore with learners, but there is no need to do this. Unpacking learning intentions is also about uncovering the possibilities for establishing the context and relevance for our learners that exists in every bit of the curriculum. In every case, we need to look closely at the language of the standard in question, whatever standard it may be, and carefully consider what it tells us.

In our example, we used unpacking questions in Chapter 2, and one of them was, 'What does *significance* mean?' The questions we pose to our learners that stem from this involve a thorough investigation of the language, and this is where we help our learners exercise agency through exploring their assumptions and personal perception. We use questions such as:

- What does it mean to be significant to the history of a country like Australia?
- What would you consider to be a significant person, group, place or event in Australia's history and why?
- What would it mean if you were considered 'insignificant' to history?
- How do we decide what is significant to a country's history and what is not?

As soon as you begin to explore these and other powerful conceptual questions with learners, they start to make connections to the curriculum that are relevant and meaningful as well as those that explore multiple perspectives on the content itself, and the whole thing springs to life for them. This also demonstrates to educators that they are not tethered to specific periods or events that can make for linear content-driven lessons. Remember from Chapter 2 that learning intentions are essential understandings, critical concepts and individual perspectives. By letting the learners take the lead, they will conduct their own topical investigations in ways that engage them. In this case, a potentially lacklustre history lesson suddenly becomes a rich unit of inquiry.

From this, one example of success criteria that could arise is challenging the learners to tell the story of Australia's history that *they* feel should have been told. This might include telling the stories of those groups that may have been considered less significant, such as women and Aboriginal and Torres Strait Islander peoples, and providing the voices for them that history may not have previously heard. Imagine the depth of research and personal insight involved in producing the historical narratives of different people and groups. Think of the creativity and critical thinking quotient for this kind of challenge. Most of all, consider how such an endeavour exercises learner agency over the learning, and all because we give learners a chance to make the learning intentions and success criteria their own.

Beyond Lesson Zero

From our foundation of Lesson Zero, we now head into Lesson One. Take a moment to consider the amount of time we waste planning to minutia dozens of lessons for a unit without considering first what the learners already know, are capable of, or are curious about. This is another significant time saving for teachers by employing Lesson Zero and a pedagogy of agency instead of a pedagogy of oppression. We only really know at the moment where our learners are, and it is from that point that we can determine what the next steps should be. As I stated in *Mindful Assessment*, 'We should not see learning as the outcome of teaching but rather allow teaching to become a mindful response to learning' (Crockett & Churches, 2017, p. 2).

Having reflected on Lesson Zero and determined the next steps, we begin our first lesson, we present the lesson objective as a purposeful activity towards the success criteria but not the broader learning intention. Through discussion with learners, we make a connection between the lesson objective, the learning intention and the success criteria. The discussion, even if it is a brief one (and it should be), helps learners understand that if they undertake a specific, purposeful activity, it moves them towards accomplishing the success criteria. If they have clarity around this, then the activity becomes purposeful.

> *We should not see learning as the outcome of teaching but rather allow teaching to become a mindful response to learning.*

Next, while things are transpiring during and at the end of the lesson, we want to refer back to the success criteria. This engages learners in an ongoing reflection on their progress and the evidence of that progress, including where they are in the learning journey and what remains to be accomplished. In this way, they are constantly considering what new success criteria they achieve, how they will demonstrate this and what their next steps will be individually and collectively.

What is important to realise here is that, with the presence of success criteria, the need for a standard examination or test becomes irrelevant. That is what mindful assessment is all about – not measuring the effectiveness of learning at an endpoint but rather establishing clear success criteria for arriving at our learning destination. And, as we already know, that criteria comes from unpacking the learning intentions.

At Lesson Zero, learners reflect on what success criteria they already meet. In other words, they are gathering evidence and demonstrating where they are in relation to the success criteria. They reflect on this progress and evidence continually as the lessons progress.

With the Lesson Zero structure, what could happen, and usually does, is that learners may arrive at the success criteria much earlier than we expect. When we present the lessons one at a time without clarifying a destination, there is definitely no chance of this happening. However, when we hand the success criteria to our learners, they already have the keys to success up front. From there, those who want to direct their learning, do extra work and really dive into the criteria have the agency to do so. What this means for the structure of our teaching is that when learners arrive at the success criteria several lessons earlier than expected, we do not need extra lessons. We have saved what every teacher says they never have enough of – time! The end of the learning is not when there are no more lessons; it is when the success criteria have been achieved. That is a crucial understanding for us in this process.

The end of the learning is not when there are no more lessons; it is when the success criteria have been achieved.

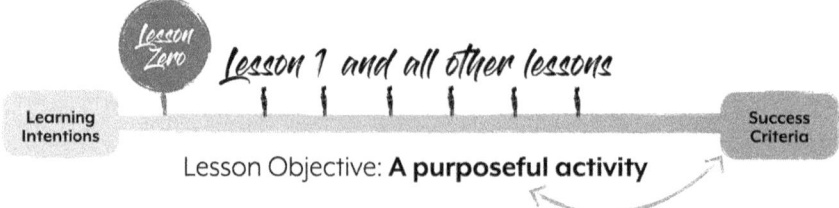

- **Lesson Objective** is presented

- Through discussion, the connection is made between **Lesson Objective**, **Learning Intentions**, and **Success Criteria**

- As appropriate, **during** and **at the end** of the lesson, **Success Criteria is referenced** for learners to **consider progress and evidence**

- **Next steps** in learning are determined collectively

Source: © 2022 by Lee Crockett, Future-Focused Learning Network, Learning Intentions 2.0 masterclass.

Figure 4.3: How lessons progress after Lesson Zero is implemented.

When we allow learners to be in charge of their learning through transparency with success criteria, they largely start to direct their learning (see figure 4.3). There is a massive appetite for this among learners. When they have the opportunity to unpack their learning and internalise the established success criteria, they excel in almost every case.

In my work with a school in Dubai, I saw plenty of confusion among the teachers as they sought to understand my explanations about learning intentions and success criteria. I quickly realised that before their first lessons even began, teachers needed a firm grasp of the Lesson Zero concept – what we do before any learning starts. One teacher, a biology teacher, taught a specific unit in Year 11 biology, which always took her exactly thirty-two lessons. What was the reason it took this long? It was because she had thirty-two planned lessons she felt needed to be executed to deliver the content, and as such, her learners had no choice but to follow the trajectory and arrive at the final lesson. As she began revisiting her approach, she used flipped learning to encourage students to independently reflect on their next steps at the end of each lesson, so they came prepared for the next one. They identified where they were in relation to success criteria and determined their next logical steps. In this first trial iteration, even with a demanding, content-heavy curriculum such as Year 11 biology, her learners arrived at their final established success criteria in sixteen lessons, a total 50 per cent reduction in instruction time. In addition to this, learner outcomes improved by 12 per cent.

What does all this mean? It means this teacher and her students now had extra time to explore specific topics more deeply or discuss issues that were relevant to the learners, and they still would continue to heighten engagement and improve learner outcomes.

This is not an isolated incident, either. I can honestly report that this has happened with every school I have worked with to introduce learning intentions and success criteria, if the teachers have embraced the approach with commitment and focus. When we initiate learning intentions and success criteria into our teaching, do it well and commit to applying Lesson Zero, amazing things can happen for our learners in developing agency and engagement in learning.

A Few Reminders About Lesson Zero

I understand that everything we have discussed is a lot for anyone to take in. Lesson Zero is an entirely new concept for many reading this, and it can initially seem overwhelming. Here are just a few reminders for you to consider:

1. A unit of learning begins with provocation and the learning intentions and ends when the success criteria have been achieved.

2. The more time you invest in making learning intentions clear, the faster your learners will achieve the success criteria and the better your outcomes will be.

3. Lesson Zero is completed before the start of any other lessons, and it takes as long as it takes.

Here is another word of advice: it is imperative that you approach the first practical application of all this with patience, compassion, humility and a sense of humour. Be patient with yourself and, above all, with your learners. In most cases, none of you will have done this before, and it is a new way of learning that requires an adjustment period. Be transparent and let them know you are learning too. It makes you human and demonstrates that not knowing is normal. Most importantly, stepping back from a position of authority provides a space for your learners to step forward into agency. Lesson Zero provides an instructional method that will empower your learners to be highly successful and begin the shift from agents to agency.

You already have everything you require to be successful with Lesson Zero. You already know what learning intentions are and how to unpack them, and you can develop success criteria to guide your learners towards meeting those intentions. The next steps are simple – give it a go with your learners and see what happens.

Summary and Key Points

- Lesson Zero happens before any other lessons begin. It is when we set up the unit of work and unpack everything with the learners.

- Lesson Zero is completed before the start of any other lessons, and it takes as long as it takes.

- There are two main elements to Lesson Zero: unpacking the learning intentions and establishing purpose and co-constructing success criteria with learners. Learners also reflect on what success criteria they have already met and determine the first steps in the learning.

- When we have success criteria, which we established while unpacking the learning intention, the need for a standard examination or test becomes irrelevant.

- With Lesson Zero, what can and often does happen is that learners arrive at the success criteria earlier than we expect, which gives us more time for additional learning and exploration.

- The more time you invest in clarifying learning intentions, the faster your learners will achieve the success criteria and the better your outcomes will be.

Guiding Questions

1. How do students know what they are learning and why?
2. What is Lesson Zero, and what is it meant to achieve for our learners?
3. How does using Lesson Zero foster learner agency?
4. What are the advantages of Lesson Zero in terms of outcome and engagement?
5. Why is it essential to let Lesson Zero take as long as necessary to accomplish?

Chapter 5

Destinations, Milestones and Footsteps

A journey of a thousand miles starts with a single step.

Lao Tzu, *Tao Te Ching*

How do we move forward consistently and increasingly foster opportunities for our learners to develop agency and give them the space they need to accomplish their goals? Think back to our conversation about momentum in the previous chapter (page 59). I stressed that for there to be momentum in learning, there must first be motion. The difficulty we face with momentum is that often our mind is focused and stuck on something or someplace other than where we truly are. Mindfulness practice, in its simplest form, is the process of recognising this as it occurs and putting our mind back in its proper place, right here and right now. In my experience, there are two main places we get lost.

The first one is when we employ the phrase *should have*. When we use this, we are referring to the past and to things that already happened, fixating on and perhaps regretting what we failed to do or say. We all have done this, and have maybe even fallen prey to an imaginary scenario we crafted in our minds in which, if we had only spoken, acted or chosen differently, we would be enjoying an alternate and entirely fictional outcome.

The other place we get stuck that prevents us from having momentum and moving forward is the little place called *could be*. Here, our imagination obsesses over what it is we want to have happen and what we want the future to look like. Often we're told that it's good to focus on dreams and to have a vision and plan for how to achieve them. The danger rests in becoming attached and fixed to these visions and exhibiting neither the willingness nor the capacity to allow any deviation. I'm sure that most of the things you've planned in your life did not turn out exactly as you had imagined, and today you are instead living some variation of your original mental picture.

Much of the planning we do as educators relates to visions and goals and the like. We must realise, because of how we've been conditioned by our experiences as well as the experiences of others, that we often have preconceived notions about how these look in practice. With strategic planning, or when creating a project plan or any other plan in your life, the process is pretty straightforward. Engineer a plan, execute the plan and hope for the best outcome.

However, we often devise 3–5-year strategic plans, the assumption being that absolutely nothing will change in those impending 3–5 years. There will be no change in government, policy or funding; there will still be the same number of employees; they will still have the same level of health; their priorities won't need to shift; there won't be a war or a global pandemic. The future is not guaranteed, and none of these assumptions is a given. In fact, they are all highly unlikely. This makes a five-year plan nothing more than a strategic wish that can easily be derailed by any unknown variables over which we have no control. The time, money and effort involved in creating a massive plan becomes a catalyst that assures its rigidity and, ultimately, its failure and abandonment in the face of adversity.

In light of this realisation, there has to be some fluidity and adaptability when making plans, which can only come from placing our focus on what we can do at the moment and being willing to pivot. It means having the same endpoint in mind but keeping the planning light enough to respond to the fundamental uncertainty with which we all live. To enable this, I would like to introduce in this chapter the three distinct areas of planning I use in my executive coaching program (available at futurefocusedlearning.net/executive-coaching) to support teams as they accelerate strategic goals while navigating real-time circumstances.

Destinations, Milestones and Footsteps: An Overview

Many of the terms we use in goal vernacular encourage a fixed mindset. Think about your association with the words *goal*, *plan*, *vision*, *strategic priorities*, *strategy*, *initiatives* and *tasks*. These are terms heavily loaded with our experiences and assumptions. In Chapter 2 (page 29), I went to great lengths to differentiate learning intentions from lesson objectives because of our experiences with these terms and our beliefs about what they mean.

I've stated previously that teams and individuals do their best, most profound and most creative work when empowered with a clarity of purpose, plan and responsibility. As I advocate in all of my work, the best approach is the simplest. Over the years, I've found that using the process of destinations, milestones and footsteps as a road map for achieving clarity of vision and purpose works more effectively than any other planning or goal-setting progression. A significant reason is the explicit imagery the terms allude to, which clarifies the process. Let's look at the definitions of each one, along with a pertinent example.

Destinations

A journey always has an endpoint, intentional or otherwise. Let's imagine we decide to hike Mt Fuji. There are four main trails to the summit, each with its characteristics. The Yoshida trail, which is the most popular, is described as a zigzag path on a relatively flat ground surface with many mountain huts, shops and public toilets. The Fujinomiya trail, on the other hand, is very rocky and steep, with few huts and one shop. Though the character of the journey is different, the destination is the same.

In a school or corporate setting, we would consider our destinations to perhaps be elements of our school improvement plan. Destinations are where most department of education strategies end. The concepts and ideals are typically unsupported by a method or measurement of success.

- ***Destinations* definition:** Places of interest expressed in general terms, concepts, or ideals.
- **Mt Fuji example:** Hike Mt Fuji.
- **Agency example:** Students have agency over their learning, demonstrating success in planning their learning and measuring their results.

Milestones

An ascent of Mt Fuji takes between five and seven hours. At some point, we want to know that we are going in the right direction and how much further we must go. On each trail, clear markers inform you that you are still on the correct course. Since the trails intersect, markers on the trails are coordinated in inscription, design and colour. Even so, at the eighth station junction, about a thousand people go down the Subashiri trail by mistake every season and cannot get back onto the Yoshida trail, so it is a significant milestone.

In our first agency scenario, the destination is expressed in general terms, concepts or ideals such as *agency over their learning* or *demonstrating success*. We need to determine, for example, how we would define *agency*, what would evidence students having agency and how we would measure success in planning their learning. These milestones must be quantifiable in the same way a trail marker designates a precise location on our journey. In other words, milestones are clearly defined and are the evidence of progress towards a destination.

- *Milestones* **definition:** Measurable points of progress or indicators of positive movement towards destinations.
- **Mt Fuji example:** The eighth station 'Shita-edoya' mountain hut.
- **Agency example:** All faculty complete the Agency masterclass, posting each session challenge and reflection, evidencing the 'Evaluating' level of the Agents to Agency Continuum.

Footsteps

The Yoshida trail is a loop of 18.7 kilometres, which equates to between 11 000 and 15 000 footsteps. It would be impossible to plan out all those steps. Further, if we happen to slide (a likely event for those on the volcanic gravel trail), our plan is invalidated. A much more reasonable and practical approach is to know the next milestone and judge the path ahead, thinking about the next few steps only and readjusting when we slide.

There is no shortage of things in a school that trip up our plans – everything from staff absentees to fire alarms to COVID-19 and lockdowns.

Destinations, Milestones and Footsteps

As I mentioned earlier, the future is unknown, so planning the next two or three footsteps makes far more sense. If the first one doesn't happen, the next 14 999 need to be adjusted; it makes more sense to know your milestones and plan the following few footsteps only, changing when you see what happens.

- *Footsteps* **definition:** Small, essential positive actions towards a milestone that must be accomplished within a specific period

- **Mt Fuji example:** (1) Turn left at the eighth station 'Shita-edoya' mountain hut. (2) Ascend the narrow trail in front of the hut.

- **Agency example:** (1) Complete session one of the Agency masterclass. (2) Collect and post evidence in the Future-Focused Learning Network. (3) Unpack results with colleagues in the PLC meeting.

These definitions, along with examples, can be seen in figure 5.1.

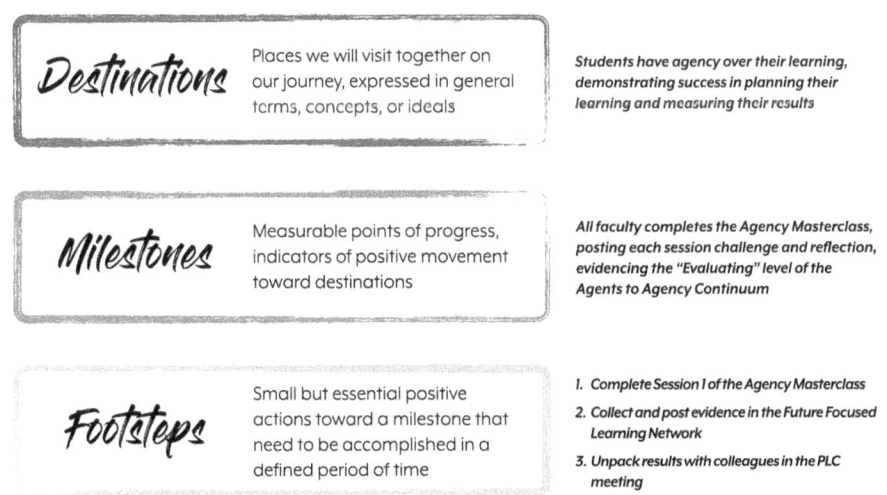

Source: © 2022 by Lee Crockett.

Figure 5.1: Exemplars of what destinations, milestones and footsteps might look like for fostering learner agency.

What I urge you to take away from this discussion is the importance of being in the moment. I tend to focus on clarity and simplicity in my work with schools and organisations worldwide. My perception has been that when teams or organisations plan a project or engineer a goal they wish to accomplish, they tend to overplan and obsess about the minutiae of the details. You never really know where you need to go next until you see where you are. As educators, we must strive to begin understanding our place in the present by being mindful of where our learners and we are now, at this moment, and stifling the urge to project too far into an unknowable future. The only moment we have absolute control over is the present one, and it is there that great things begin.

After determining where we are, the next thing we need to know is where we're going and what our next few steps are. We don't need to know the next thousand or ten thousand steps but simply the next two or three. In this case, whether I'm consulting with a school administration, working with a company or even conferring with my team to move projects forward, I adhere to a strict set of principles that allow any group to thrive and accomplish amazing things. Generally, I recommend that a team allows itself to have two destinations at a time and limits milestones to a projected timeframe of no more than six weeks. That means no five-year plan, three-year plan or even one-year plan – it means a plan only for the upcoming few weeks (see figure 5.2 for an example).

Why does this work? Because limiting project planning to only two destinations at a time achieves the clarity and simplicity I mentioned earlier and usually, by extension, a stronger focus, a clearer vision and end goal, and highly achievable, realistic outcomes. A simplified approach such as this allows a team to consider the question, 'Are we working on A, or are we working on B?' And if we're not working on either one, we should perhaps climb out of the rabbit hole we've fallen into and start working on either A or B.

Milestones, if you recall, are the measurable points of progress; thus, they are our success criteria. From this we know that if we have reached all our milestones, we've arrived at our destination. There is no limit to the number of milestones you can have, but they must be measurable and of a single scope.

If you're used to long-term planning, this kind of looser structure might make you think, 'Well, if you only have two or three things to do, how are you going to stay on track, and how are you going to continue to move forward, and what will you do when you run out of those things?' I would address this by saying the advantage here is that because it's not a plan that was created and is sitting in a drawer or a giant document somewhere, and because it's a living plan or sprint of only a few weeks, we're constantly focused on it. There's no danger of the plan being tucked away out of sight somewhere and forgotten about.

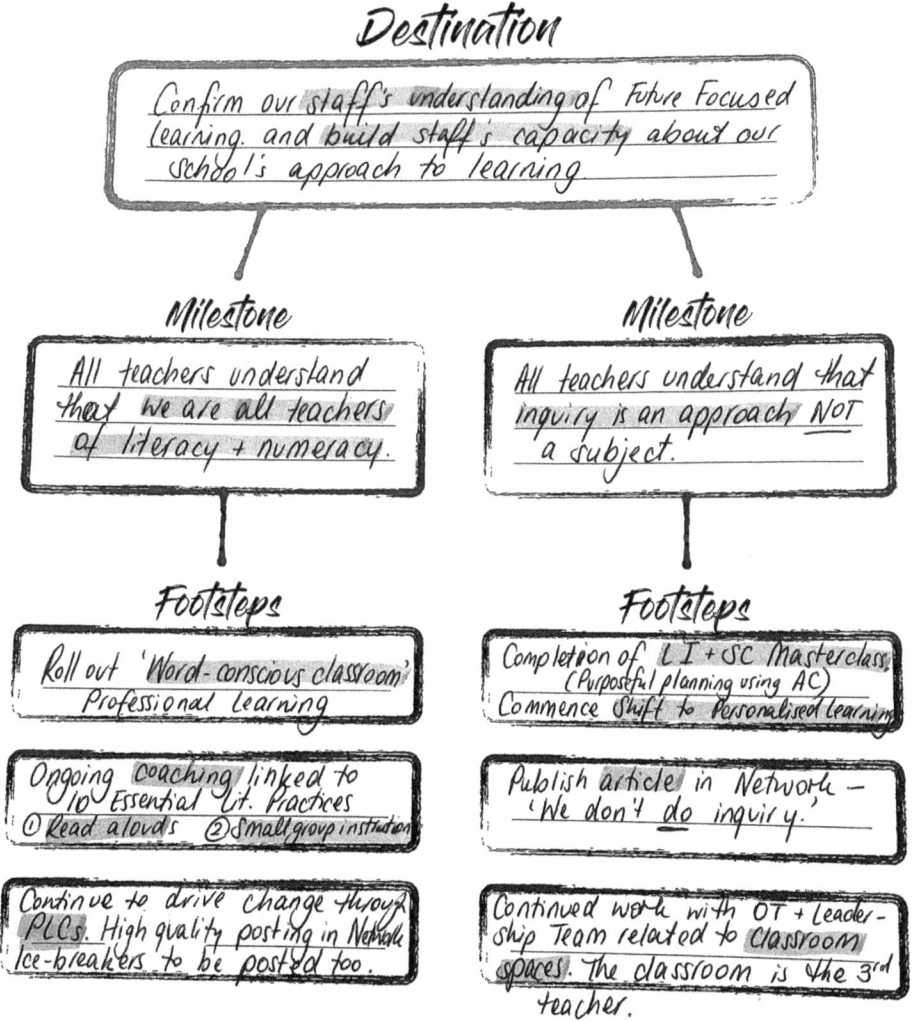

Source: © 2022 by Evelyn Scott School. Used with permission.

Figure 5.2: Senior leadership team's plan for a six-week sprint.

At this point, you're likely wondering how all this ties into the cultivation of learner agency. Simply put, supporting learners to create personalised footsteps and milestones to guide their learning is a sure way to cultivate agency. Encouraging learners to have agency and responsibility for their learning journeys is the key to helping them succeed.

Goal Setting and Agency

Perhaps the most effective means for helping learners develop responsibility and agency over their learning is to engage them in the regular application of setting goals. As humans, we possess the inherent ability and fortitude to regulate our lives through the consistent application of purposeful thought (Bandura et al., 1999). When it comes to thinking purposefully about goals and how to achieve them, we can do an excellent service to our learners by teaching them how to effectively set goals.

There are thousands of studies pointing to clear evidence of the impact of setting goals, some of which we'll be referencing in the following section. For example, one study on academic achievement indicates that outcomes improve by as much as 30 per cent just by goal setting (Morisano, 2013), and the effect on wellbeing is substantial. It doesn't even matter if the goals aren't academic – simply the act of defining and thinking clearly about personal goals affects academic achievement (Morisano et al., 2010).

Goal setting is not a new method for achieving success. In fact, it appeared back in the time of ancient Greece in the writings of Aristotle and Plato. For example, in their philosophies on final causality, they suggest having a purpose incites one to take action (Lawlor & Hornyak, 2012). As discussed in Chapter 1 (page 11), agency refers to autonomy over learning. Among other things, learning autonomy calls for the self-determination of goals and how the learner can best achieve them. Self-determination describes an individual's capacity to 'act as the primary causal agents in one's life and to maintain or improve one's quality of life' (Wehmeyer, 2005, p. 117). Individuals who exhibit self-determination have a higher quality of life in areas such as gainful employment, postsecondary education opportunities, independent living and community involvement (Shogren et al., 2017). From this, it's easy to see how self-determination can also easily apply to the quality of one's learning and one's goals for education.

In most conditions, goals that are both specific and challenging tend to yield more favourable results for the goal setter than general, nonspecific goals (Locke & Latham, 2002). This makes sense when aligned with our earlier discussion about clarity – knowing where you are and where you're going, how you'll get there and how you'll know you arrived.

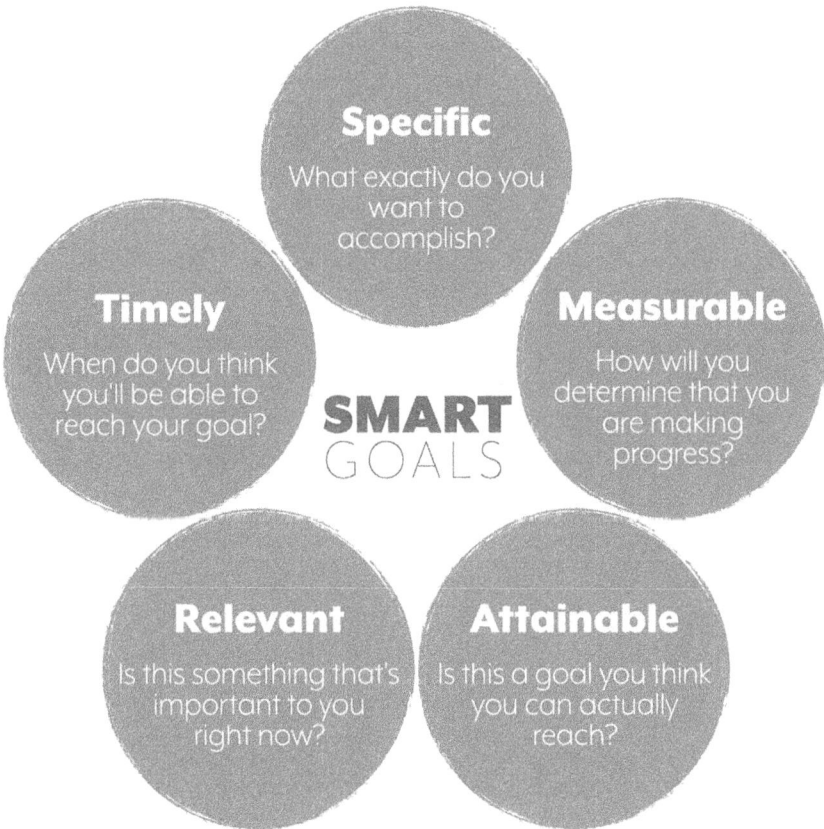

Figure 5.3: SMART goals.

By now, you have probably heard of the term *SMART goals*. The acronym SMART, as it applies to goal setting, has a somewhat vague history. Still, its genesis is often attributed to George Doran (1981). The expanded acronym can be seen in figure 5.3, with the five elements as follows:

- **Specific.** What exactly do you want to accomplish? How particular can you be about the details?

- **Measurable.** How will you determine that you are making progress? How will you know when you've reached your goal?
- **Attainable.** Is this a goal you think you can reach? Do you have the resources necessary to achieve this goal? If not, how will you obtain them?
- **Relevant.** Is this important to you right now? Why is this goal significant to you?
- **Timely.** When do you think you'll be able to reach your goal? Is your timeframe realistic enough?

Above all, the SMART goal-setting system allows learners to define attainable goals because they are specific and measurable and, therefore, more likely to foster accountability and engagement. Some examples of SMART goals compared to ones that are less specific can be seen in table 5.1.

Table 5.1: A comparison of SMART and non-SMART goals.

Non-SMART Goals	SMART Goals
Practise writing every day.	Devote a 15-minute time block to writing every evening, focusing on structured journalling.
Study more often.	Dedicate 2 hours to study twice each week for the entire year, removing all distractions, and using a planner to keep track of time and focus topics.
Become more involved in school activities.	Choose and sign up for an extracurricular activity before the end of autumn.
Apply for university.	Set out course preferences and lodge applications before the due date.

Source: Adapted from Estrapala & Reed, 2019.

In addition to the SMART considerations, it can also be helpful to consider other questions, such as:

- What are the benefits of achieving this goal for me?
- What is my primary motivation?
- What will I do if things don't go as planned or something derails my progress?
- What will my next steps be after this?

With the use of SMART goals, it's assured that 'students have enough information and specificity to monitor and evaluate their progress toward attaining the goal and improving their academic outcomes' (Estrapala & Reed, 2019, p. 287). If you look closely at the SMART goal-setting structure, you can see how it fits with a framework for fostering learner agency. Learners employ a SMART strategy when unpacking learning intentions, crafting success criteria and determining their personal learning goals. The SMART strategy also comes into play when learners work in teams to increase accountability across group members and adhere to a unified team vision. Committing to specific, measurable, attainable and relevant goals for learning causes learners to instinctively direct their focus towards achieving those goals while also disengaging in behaviours such as lack of attention, noncompliance and other conduct that can hinder constructive learning experiences (Locke, 1996).

Supporting learners to create personalised footsteps and milestones to guide their learning is a sure way to cultivate agency.

Research tells us that goal setting provides lasting benefits both in and beyond school and is also a critical factor in advancing learner agency. A study of undergraduate students at McGill University determined that the process of guiding learners in setting personal or academic goals improves their academic outcomes (Morisano et al., 2010). After a four-month trial, the study concluded that 'students who completed the goal-setting intervention displayed significant improvements in academic performance compared with the control group' (Morisano et al., 2010).

Another notable study at the University of Rotterdam involves two groups of first-year university learners who were measured on academic performance, with one group being a control group and the other using goal-setting approaches (Schippers et al., 2020). The study's findings demonstrate that the goal-setting group showed a greater than 20 per cent increase in academic performance compared to the control group (Schippers et al., 2020). The positive effects of successful goal setting are not limited to performance in school, either. Another study concludes that 'the ability to establish and maintain appropriate goals and commitments appears to be integral to development throughout adulthood' (Holahan, 1988, p. 286).

How Learners Can Start Setting Goals

If learners have agency over personalised goal setting, the potential it has for positively affecting continuous engagement with learning, academic goals and academic performance is significant (Yusuff, 2018). However, as with all new skills, learners need a starting point, and we covered this in Chapter 2 when we discussed learning intentions. You'll find that the process for goal setting runs parallel to the learning intention unpacking process, which we're already familiar with.

For our purposes here, we're going to propose three main areas for learners to get started with goal setting, which is simply another way of describing the process of unpacking a learning intention (see figure 5.4):

1. **Self-determination:** Where are we and what do we want to accomplish? (learning intention)
2. **Self-regulation:** How will we get there? (lesson objectives)
3. **Self-assessment:** How will we know we succeeded and what are the next steps? (success criteria)

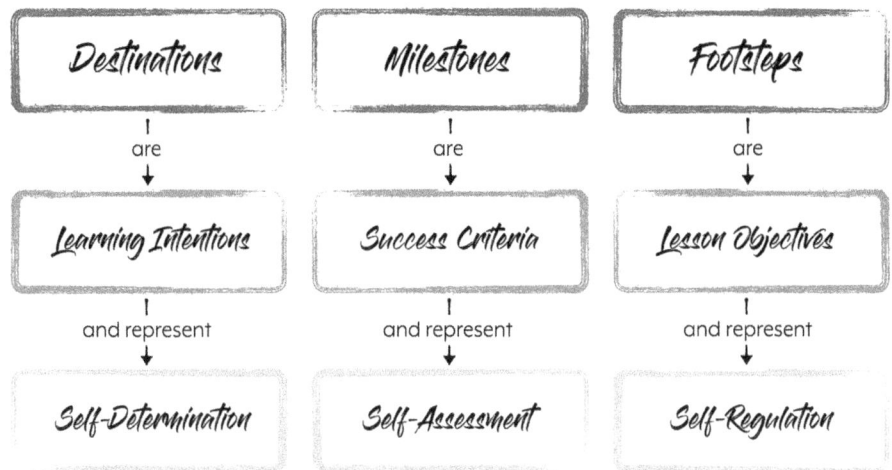

Figure 5.4: How destinations, milestones and footsteps are related to learning intentions, lesson objectives and success criteria.

Self-Determination

Goal setting begins when learners decide exactly what they want to accomplish and specify the end goal, including an approximate timeframe for achievement if desired. This is the realm of *self-determination*, which one study describes as an individual's capacity to 'act as the primary causal agents in one's life and to maintain or improve one's quality of life' (Wehmeyer, 2005, p. 117). Individuals who exhibit self-determination have a higher quality of life in areas such as gainful employment, postsecondary education opportunities, independent living and community involvement (Shogren et al., 2017). Learners begin the goal-setting process by using self-determination to establish purpose, which means clearly keeping the end in mind. This is the destination they want to reach, and it is defined by the milestones they realistically set for achievement.

Questions for learners to ask regarding self-determination include:

- What is my goal?
- How specific can I be about what I want to achieve?
- Can I realistically achieve this goal?
- Why is this important to me?

- What is my strongest motivating factor?
- When do I want to accomplish this?
- How can I reinforce my goal (writing it down, repeating it aloud daily and so on)?
- Who can help me if I need it?

Self-Regulation

The simplest definition of *self-regulation* is 'the ability to act in your long-term best interest, consistent with your deepest values' (para. 1, Stosny, 2011). Think of self-regulation as the enactment of the learning objectives and the footsteps in the journey. Learners with agency over learning goals must have every opportunity possible to self-regulate their progressive steps towards achieving the footsteps and milestones they create. As one study suggests, the vast majority of popular theories about self-regulation recognise its inherent link to goal setting, adding that 'goals enhance self-regulation through their effects on motivation, learning, self-efficacy (perceived capabilities for learning or performing actions at given levels), and self-evaluations of progress' (Schunk, 2001, p. 1).

Questions for learners to ask regarding self-regulation include:
- What steps will I take to get there?
- How will I monitor progress?
- Do my action consistently reflect my desire to achieve my goal?
- What might be getting in my way?
- What will I do if something gets in my way?
- What can I do to get to my destination faster?
- Do I need to readjust my milestones and deadlines?

Self-Assessment

There's no question that for progress to be meaningful, it must be assessed somehow; this is especially true for setting goals. If we want to promote learner agency as much as possible, I maintain that we must involve students in the development, application and reporting of their learning assessment. The truth is that when we let students assess themselves, there is a great potential for them to experience more pride in their learning, a heightened sense of ownership of their efforts and increased higher-order thinking capacity. Moreover, with the best self-assessment practices, the teacher has the most crucial role as the moderator of the assessment (Crockett, 2019). If a learner properly develops the faculty for assessing their own goals through consistent independent practice, they can contribute much to the development of their agency over learning.

Questions for learners to ask regarding self-assessment include:

- Did I achieve my goal and meet my success criteria?
- If not, what went wrong, and what can I do differently?
- What are my next steps?

Since learning should always have a purpose, this means having the end clearly in mind. There must be a valid and worthwhile reason for the learning. To have any value, it must be a meaningful and valuable experience we can move forward in our lives. This is especially true for our learners, and goal setting is one of those lifelong learning skills that can build learner agency while strengthening the *desire* to learn.

Agency Through Destinations, Milestones and Footsteps

Studies indicate that complexity of a goal is not necessarily a hindering factor in goal achievement, as the goals learners set for themselves affect their performances through causal mechanisms. This means learners who are enthusiastic about their goals tend to instinctively place their focus and effort on goal-relevant activities while avoiding actions not related to the achievement of those goals (Locke & Latham, 1990; Smith et al., 1990). As long as the goals are relevant and meaningful to the learner, goals inspire a level of effort and persistence likely to be congruent with how challenging they are to achieve. In the McGill University study mentioned previously, Morisano (2013) asserts that 'in the cognitive realm, goals motivate people to recall or discover task strategies that facilitate goal achievement' (p. 496). Furthermore, in most cases, 'goals that are both specific and challenging tend to yield more favourable results for the goal-setter than that of general, non-specific goals' (Locke & Latham, 2002, p. 708).

The concepts of destinations, milestones and footsteps transfer easily to learners. They are not complex structures and allow learners to succeed quickly. Simply put, the destinations are learning intentions, the milestones are the success criteria and the footsteps are lesson objectives or individual actions. Figure 5.5 shows examples of destinations, milestones and footsteps from a Year 4 mathematics class.

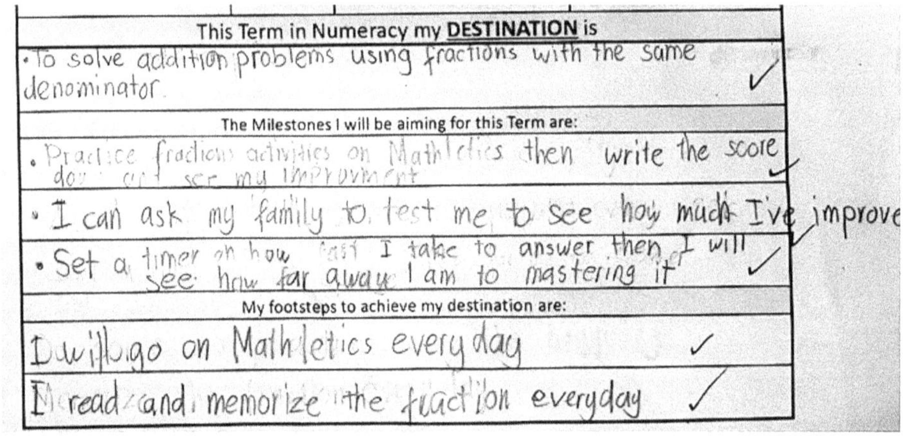

This Term in Numeracy my **DESTINATION** is
• To solve addition problems using fractions with the same denominator. ✓
The Milestones I will be aiming for this Term are:
• Practice fractions activities on Mathletics then write the score down and see my improvement ✓
• I can ask my family to test me to see how much I've improve ✓
• Set a timer on how fast I take to answer then I will see how far away I am to mastering it ✓
My footsteps to achieve my destination are:
I will go on Mathletics every day ✓
I read and memorize the fraction everyday ✓

Source: © 2022 by Lalor Primary School. Used with permission.

Figure 5.5: Exemplars of destinations, milestones and footsteps crafted by Year 4 learners at Lalor Primary School.

One final note about learning goals, destinations, milestones and footsteps: please keep at the forefront of your mind the two things I mentioned earlier – *clarity* and *simplicity*. It is only by having a clearly defined destination or intention that our learners will be able to achieve it. It is through the implementation of a simple yet engaging approach to learning that they are more likely to adhere to the journey until the very end, when they can look back at their progress in self-reflection and proclaim, 'I did it!'

Summary and Key Points

- Successful planning requires clarity and simplicity, and a desire to act in the moment while maintaining forward momentum.
- The simplest and most effective way to plan for success is by using destinations, milestones and footsteps.
- Learner agency is highly influenced by a learner's ability to engage in successful goal setting, especially using SMART goals.
- Thousands of studies indicate that effective goal setting can dramatically improve academic performance and success in adulthood beyond school.
- The process of goal setting mirrors the same process we use to unpack a learning intention.

Guiding Questions

1. How does momentum apply to successful learning and especially to fostering learner agency?
2. Why do destinations, milestones and footsteps matter to learner agency?
3. How do we achieve clarity of purpose?
4. What does it mean to have goals?
5. Why is goal setting one of the most profoundly beneficial things we can teach our learners?
6. How can we teach our learners how to set goals?

Chapter 6

Progressions to Self-Directed Learner Agency

O this learning, what a thing it is!

William Shakespeare, *The Taming of the Shrew*

When I returned to high school with the encouragement of my teacher, my learning environment was extremely unusual – I was essentially left to my own devices, with occasional input from my teacher if I directly sought it. While this particular educational experience worked for me, we have established throughout this book that learner agency is not an individual effort and that it is best developed as co-agency, with facilitated support from the educator. In fact, it would be irresponsible to just throw learners into this without guidance. Both teachers and learners need scaffolding and measurable points of progress in the transition from agents to agency.

This chapter presents a series of continuums from my Future-Focused Learning Network Agents to Agency masterclass (available at futurefocusedlearning.net). These resources guide educators to support learners to take agency as they develop the knowledge, skills and dispositions to work independently. The levels align with Bloom's revised taxonomy. Moving through Bloom's is itself moving from passive to agentic thinking. It is the perfect example of agency as both the characteristic of learning and the outcome of it. However, you will notice I have supplemented Bloom's categories with an additional two levels – (1) awareness and (2) connection – and I'll explain why.

Awareness is necessary at the commencement of the learning process, as learners cannot remember something they are not aware of – they first must have awareness of its existence. As facilitators of learning, we focus on creating awareness and stimulating connection because these have the most impact on potential depth of learning.

Once we become fully aware of something, our connection to it determines which of Bloom's taxonomic levels our learning has the potential to reach. For example, if there is a low level of connection, learners will likely not achieve much beyond remembering or understanding. However, if there exists a high level of connection, learning has the potential to involve taxonomic levels all the way up to evaluating and creating.

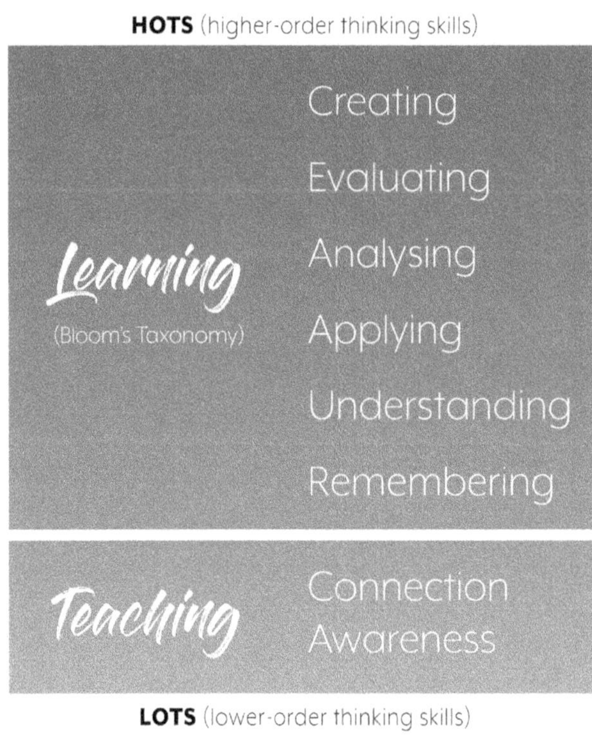

HOTS (higher-order thinking skills)

Learning
(Bloom's Taxonomy)

Creating
Evaluating
Analysing
Applying
Understanding
Remembering

Teaching

Connection
Awareness

LOTS (lower-order thinking skills)

Figure 6.1: The eight levels of Agents to Agency.

Progressions to Self-Directed Learner Agency

Figure 6.1 illustrates how these new levels fit in with Bloom's revised taxonomy of thinking skills to comprise the eight levels of the Agents to Agency pathway. The gap between connection and remembering indicates the transition from teaching to learning. The taxonomic levels, from remembering to creating, are learning as they occur *within the learner*. The depth of the learning, however, is a result of the strength of connection created through the teaching experience. For this reason, provocation, learning intentions and creating a strong level of engagement for the learner are critical.

The following sections describe the levels of Agents to Agency. They present criteria that would indicate evidence that a teacher is at this level and, specifically, what a teacher is not doing at this level. Each section also details criteria showing evidence of learner behaviours indicative of each level.

The levels are not a reflection of you as a teacher or what you are doing right or wrong. I believe there is no such thing as best practice; there is only evolving practice. I mentioned in the introduction that a measurable, transparent process is required for success of any initiative. You can use this continuum to reflect on where your practice and your learners are now and consider the next logical steps in the evolution from Agents to Agency.

Agents to Agency Level 1 - Awareness

At the lowest level level, the teacher is aware of the content and the learners' expected progressions within the curriculum. They develop individual lessons with outcomes based on content and state the aim or purpose. They know where they are going with the lesson and how to present this with clarity.

The learners have no role in crafting the learning intentions, success criteria, lesson progressions or assessments. Therefore, learners are strictly agents of the teacher.

This level is evidenced when the teacher:

- develops lessons based on curricular content
- states some form of aim or purpose of the lesson with clarity
- uses WALT or WILT to describe intent, purpose, or success

- states task completion as the goal of the lesson
- evaluates completed tasks.

This level is *not* evidenced when the teacher:

- engages in direct or explicit instruction without clearly articulating the aim or purpose of the lesson
- develops the lesson as an activity or task without reference to curriculum content.

This level is evidenced when the learner:

- is aware of the stated aim or purpose of the lesson
- is unaware of success criteria and how it may be achieved
- is unaware of a learning intention beyond the scope of the lesson.

Agents to Agency Level 2 – Connection

At this level, the teacher has established a connection to the critical concepts and essential understandings behind the content of the curriculum. They connect lesson development to the critical concepts and essential understandings as the purpose of learning and have considered how learners may demonstrate success. Importantly, the teacher understands that learning intentions describe what learners must learn, distinct from what activities they want the learners to complete.

The learners continue to have no role in crafting the learning intentions, success criteria, lesson progressions or assessments. As the teacher presents a correctly formed learning intention, although the learners remain agents of the teacher, they can potentially reflect on the learning intention's meaning and consider what may constitute success.

This level is evidenced when the teacher:

- identifies the critical concepts and essential understandings within the curriculum to develop lessons
- clearly articulates a learning intention, including an essential understanding or critical concept from the curriculum

- states a learning intention as the goal of the lesson
- connects lesson development to essential understandings or critical concepts as the purpose of learning
- considers how learners may demonstrate success
- evaluates completed work against the stated learning intention.

This level is *not* evidenced when the teacher:

- states a learning intention based only on content, without connection to essential understandings or critical concepts
- states no learning intention or a learning intention as an activity or task.

This level is evidenced when the learner:

- is aware of the stated learning intention from the curriculum
- is unaware of success criteria and how success may be achieved.

Agents to Agency Level 3 - Remembering

At this level, the learning intention, based on critical learning concepts and essential understandings within the curriculum, is visible, either in written or visual form. The teacher describes the learning intention to the class and considers the learning itself as the valued goal, which may consist of a combination of knowledge, skills or big ideas; a connection to a previous lesson or prior learning; or an explanation of why this is important. The teacher explains the learning intention with clarity, checks for learner understanding through questioning and considers how they might assess learning.

The learners continue to have no role in crafting the learning intentions, success criteria, lesson progressions or assessments, remaining agents of the teacher. As the teacher has explained a correctly formed learning intention with clarity, the learners have clarity, can reflect on its meaning and form an understanding of what constitutes success.

This level is evidenced when the teacher:

- decides on appropriate and challenging learning intentions based on critical concepts and essential understandings within the curriculum and designs lessons that will enable learners to achieve them
- makes the learning intention visible to the learners in written or visual form
- explains the learning intention with clarity, checking for learner clarity through questioning
- explains the importance of the learning, establishing or articulating its purpose
- describes success in general terms
- considers the learning itself to be the valued goal
- has considered how learning may be assessed
- evaluates completed work against the stated learning intention.

This level is *not* evidenced when the teacher:

- articulates learning intentions without making them visible and accessible to learners
- does not use questioning to ensure clarity
- is unsure of the goal of the learning or how it will be assessed.

This level is evidenced when the learner:

- is able to access the learning intention throughout the lesson
- responds to questions to clearly articulate the learning intention
- is unaware of success criteria and how it may be achieved.

Agents to Agency Level 4 - Understanding

At this level, the teacher understands that learning intentions may be grouped and that most learning intentions take a series of lessons or unit to attain. They are clear on how learners will demonstrate success. They set challenging and appropriate learning goals for the group and individual learners. They engage learners in establishing purpose by clarifying the language and meaning of learning intentions through conversation, using unpacking and purposeful questions. They identify cross-curricular opportunities to merge with the current learning. They know and demonstrate strategies for initiating and managing learner discussions. They provide clearly defined success criteria that demonstrably evidence the learning intention.

The learners continue to have no role in crafting the learning intentions, success criteria, lesson progressions or assessments, remaining agents of the teacher. However, through reflecting on and responding to unpacking and purposeful questions, learners understand the meaning of the learning intention. As the teacher has provided clearly defined success criteria, learners can begin to exercise agency by working towards success criteria independent of offered lessons.

This level is evidenced when the teacher:

- presents the learning intention or intentions as an endpoint for a series of lessons or unit
- asks unpacking questions to unpack the language of the learning intention
- asks purposeful questions to investigate the meaning of the learning intention and identify cross-curricular opportunities
- uses conversation to firmly establish purpose
- provides clearly defined success criteria
- sets challenging and appropriate learning goals for the group and individual learners
- has determined clearly how learners will demonstrate success.

This level is *not* evidenced when the teacher:

- tells the learner what the learning intention means
- challenges the learner to come up with the 'right' answer
- overly controls the conversation around unpacking and herding questions, effectively limiting it to a question-and-answer session.

This level is evidenced when the learner:

- responds to questioning by sharing their thoughts, wonderings and critical reflections on the language and meaning of the learning intention
- can clearly articulate the learning intention, responding to questions to explain their understanding of the language and meaning of the learning intention
- can clearly articulate the learning goals of the group or their individual goals as set by the teacher
- can clearly articulate the purpose, from their perspective, based on their understanding of the learning intention
- understands the learning intention is an endpoint in a series of lessons
- can accurately state the success criteria.

Agents to Agency Level 5 - Applying

At this level, the teacher understands that critical learning concepts and essential understandings have personal relevance for learners and, as a result, uniquely individual perspectives. Through provocation, they inspire learner interest and curiosity in the lesson, unit or series of studies. The provocation typically precedes the presentation and unpacking of learning intentions and may connect to essential questions and global concepts. The teacher facilitates discussion to build a deeper understanding of the learning intentions and ways learners could demonstrate successful learning. They build trust and fairness through transparency about what is required and how to achieve success. The teacher co-constructs group success criteria with input from learners, engaging them by identifying personal relevance and purpose.

Although learners have no role in crafting the learning intentions, lesson progressions, or assessments, they have input into the co-construction of group success criteria and have a deeper understanding of how to achieve success. They are well positioned to work towards success criteria independent of offered lessons. As a result, they have begun the transition from agents to agency.

This level is evidenced when the teacher:

- connects learning intentions to the individual perspectives, interests and experiences of learners
- introduces learning through provocation or an essential question prior to the learning intention to inspire learner curiosity in critical concepts, essential understandings and individual perspectives
- invites every learner to respond from their own perspective, cultural background, prior experience and ability level
- engages learners by identifying their personal relevance and purpose
- co-constructs success criteria with learners, clarifying the connection to the learning intentions
- models the design of challenging, meaningful goals as a guide for learners, explicitly teaching goal setting
- shares examples of success and is transparent about how learners can achieve it.

This level is *not* evidenced when the teacher:

- presents their ideas about the importance of the learning to learners
- presents the learning intention without provocation
- presents the group with learning intentions and success criteria without modelling the process through discussion and collaboration.

This level is evidenced when the learner:

- engages in the discussion about the learning intentions, responding from their perspective
- shares prior knowledge through conversation with the group
- shares ideas and provides input to build group success criteria
- engages in activities to learn and practise goal setting

- self-assesses diagnostically by connecting to prior knowledge and experience
- understands the success criteria and is able to articulate how they will know they are successful.

Agents to Agency Level 6 – Analysing

At this level, the teacher understands what success looks like in relation to critical concepts and essential understandings beyond knowledge and skills across multiple learning areas and year levels of the curriculum. They co-create relevant and challenging learning goals through which learners connect to individual purpose, inspiring investment in their learning. They engage learners in building shared success criteria based on learning intentions and in planning a logical sequence of success criteria so that learners are actively involved in programming the group journey. They present lesson objectives as purposeful tasks that facilitate learning and make demonstrable progress towards success criteria. Through discussion, the teacher and learners make a clear connection between lesson objectives, learning intentions and success criteria. The teacher actively listens for information about what learners already know to determine what strategies to use to best engage, encourage and help each learner achieve the learning intentions. The teacher asks practical reflection questions to support the learners' realisations of what they have learned and what they need to learn next. These questions extend beyond content to thinking skills, personal growth and social responsibility.

Learners have an active role in the construction of success criteria and challenging learning goals. They understand what success looks like and where they are in relation to success. Further, they can determine the next logical progression in programming. The purpose has become transparent as there is a strong understanding of the relationship between learning intentions, success criteria and lesson objectives. Though learning intentions are prescribed and success criteria are based on the group, learners have a reasonable amount of agency over their learning.

This level is evidenced when the teacher:

- consistently asks learners to determine the next logical steps in learning
- presents clear lesson objectives as purposeful activities towards success criteria based on the steps determined by the learners
- engages learners in regular discussion to connect lesson objectives, learning intentions and success criteria
- actively listens for information about what learners already know to determine what strategies to use to best engage, encourage and help each learner
- guides the co-construction of relevant and challenging learning goals through which learners connect to individual purpose
- facilitates the construction of success criteria driven by the learners
- engages in formative assessment practices, supports learners to assess as learning and teaches the skills of self- and peer-assessment.

This level is *not* evidenced when the teacher:

- provides success criteria or offers the majority of success criteria to learners for consideration
- delivers a prescribed, predetermined program of lessons
- assesses after learning, without opportunity for learners to consider progress and evidence against success criteria
- provides more answers than questions or dominates the conversations.

This level is evidenced when the learner:

- supports the group's learning through the development of shared learning intentions and success criteria
- can identify the lesson objective and can explain how it relates to the learning intentions and success criteria of the unit of learning
- constructs relevant and challenging learning goals
- reflects on their learning in relation to the learning intentions

- reflects as a group on progress and evidence of learning in relation to success criteria
- collectively determines the next logical steps in learning
- responds individually to reflective questions, identifying and articulating what they have learned and what should next be learned
- is able to self-assess and peer-assess.

Agents to Agency Level 7 – Evaluating

At this level, the teacher guides learners through class discussion and questioning to determine personalised and shared learning intentions and success criteria, enabling them to construct individual goals and support the learning of the group. Learning intentions span multiple learning areas and year levels to meet the needs of the learners. The teacher knows learners' individual strengths and needs, building learners' confidence in their capacity to achieve goals through ongoing feedback and reflection. They understand how to engage learners in self-reflection that will support them to self-assess and plan the next logical steps. They provide timely feedback to enable learners to refine goals and next steps. The teacher understands that assessment is also feedback for the teacher and thus makes decisions about the teaching of learning strategies and processes based on the needs of the learners.

Learners are responsible for developing individual and group learning intentions and success criteria, self-assessing and determining the next logical steps and refining goals. Though the teacher provides significant support, learners have agency over their learning.

This level is evidenced when the teacher:

- engages learners in self-reflection to support self-assessment and to determine the next logical steps in programming
- facilitates individual and group learning conversations in response to learner and group needs
- provides opportunities for learners to discuss and collaborate on the learning strategies and processes they use

- supports learners to achieve goals through timely and appropriate individual feedback
- supports learners to establish purpose through the construction of challenging, relevant and measurable individual goals
- supports learners in the development of personalised and shared learning intentions and success criteria
- engages learners in self-assessment and evidence collection.

This level is *not* evidenced when the teacher:

- provides or assigns the next step in programming
- presents content or group instruction not in direct response to individual or group needs.

This level is evidenced when the learner:

- directs their learning by identifying their pathway to success criteria
- actively asks questions that drive their learning and seeks feedback or support
- can self-assess, self-report and peer-assess throughout the unit of learning and reflect on their learning individually and as a group
- creates personalised success criteria relating to individual learning goals
- engages in creating shared success criteria to support the learning of the group
- reflects on feedback and applies new thinking to achieve their goals or next steps in learning.

Agents to Agency Level 8 – Creating

At this level, the teacher understands that all learners are on their own unique learning pathway and must have their individual learning plan driven by individual purpose. The learners identify and develop the learning intentions and success criteria determined by their individual pathways, which will span multiple learning areas and potentially year levels, in addition to their learning goals and those of the group. Notably, the teacher supports learners in setting, reflecting on and evaluating academic and personal goals. They model an effective learner's behaviour, dispositions and responses using a shared language of learning. The teacher responds to learner requests for feedback by providing direction and guidance to support the learners' growth. The teacher designs the learning environment with learners and provides resources to support learner engagement, collaboration and self-efficacy.

Learners are responsible for all aspects of their learning, including learning intentions, success criteria, academic and personal goals, programming, evidence collection, assessment and reporting, as well as the learning itself. Learners have complete agency over their learning.

This level is evidenced when the teacher:

- supports learners in the development and evolution of their individual learning plans
- connects learners with relevant learning opportunities beyond the scope of the classroom or school
- discusses learning with the learner as a facilitator and mentor, responding to learner requests for support or guidance
- supports learners in the identification of appropriate learning intentions and the development of measurable success criteria
- supports learners in the establishment and refinement of academic and personal goals
- supports learners in ensuring goals, learning plan and purpose are in alignment
- supports learners to develop a reporting schema to present their evidence of learning against required outcomes.

This level is *not* evidenced when the teacher:

- engages in knowledge delivery.

This level is evidenced when the learner:

- develops and evolves a personalised learning plan

- discusses learning with facilitators and mentors, proactively seeking support, guidance and relevant learning opportunities beyond the scope of the classroom or school
- creates personalised and shared learning intentions and success criteria based on their individualised pathway
- sets challenging individual learning and personal goals, ensuring goals, learning plan and purpose are in alignment
- plans and develops a reporting schema to produce, collate, self-assess and present evidence of their learning against required outcomes.

A summary of these levels and their evidences for teachers and learners, respectively, can be seen in tables 6.1 and 6.2 (pages 116–119).

Agents to Agency continuum for teachers.

	Level 1 Awareness	Level 2 Connection	Level 3 Remembering	Level 4 Understanding	Level 5 Applying	Level 6 Analysing	Level 7 Evaluating	Level 8 Creating
Learning Foundation	Develops lessons based on curricular content.	Identifies the critical concepts and essential understandings within the curriculum to develop lessons.	Decides on appropriate and challenging learning intentions based on critical concepts and essential understandings within the curriculum and designs lessons that will enable learners to achieve them.	Presents the learning intention or intentions as an endpoint for a series of lessons or unit.	Connects learning intentions to the individual perspectives, interests and experiences of learners.	Consistently asks learners to determine the next logical steps in learning. Presents clear lesson objectives as purposeful activities towards success criteria based on the steps determined by the learners.	Engages learners in self-reflection to support self-assessment and to determine next logical steps in programming.	Supports learners in the development and evolution of their individual learning plan. Connects learners with relevant learning opportunities beyond the scope of the classroom or school.
Learning Conversation	States some form of aim or purpose of the lesson with clarity. Uses WALT and WILT to describe intent, purpose or success.	Clearly articulates a learning intention in the form of an essential understanding or critical concept from the curriculum.	Makes the learning intention visible to the learners, either in written or visual form. Explains the learning intention with clarity, checking for learner clarity through questioning.	Asks unpacking questions to unpack the language of the learning intention. Asks purposeful questions to investigate the meaning of the learning intention and identify cross-curricular opportunities.	Introduces learning through provocation or an essential question prior to the learning intention to inspire learner curiosity in critical concepts, essential understandings and individual perspectives. Invites every learner to respond from their own perspective, cultural background, prior experience and ability level.	Engages learners in regular discussion to connect lesson objectives, learning intentions and success criteria. Actively listens for information about what learners already know to determine what strategies to use to best engage, encourage and help each learner.	Facilitates individual and group learning conversations in response to learner and group needs. Provides opportunities for learners to discuss and collaborate on the learning strategies and processes they use. Supports learners to achieve goals through timely and appropriate individual feedback.	Discusses learning with the learner as a facilitator and mentor, responding to learner requests for support or guidance.

Purpose	States some form of aim or purpose of the lesson with clarity. Uses WALT and WILT to describe intent, purpose or success.	Connects lesson development to essential understandings or critical concepts as the purpose of learning.	Explains the importance of the learning, establishing or articulating its purpose.	Uses conversation to firmly establish purpose.	Engages learners by identifying their personal relevance and purpose.	Guides the co-construction of relevant and challenging learning goals through which learners connect to individual purpose.	Supports learners to establish purpose through the construction of challenging, relevant and measurable individual goals.	Supports learners in ensuring goals, learning plan and purpose are in alignment.
Success Criteria	States some form of aim or purpose of the lesson with clarity. Uses WALT and WILT to describe intent, purpose or success.	Considers how success may be demonstrated.	Describes success in general terms.	Provides clearly defined success criteria.	Co-constructs success criteria with learners, clarifying the connection to the learning intentions.	Facilitates the construction of success criteria driven by the learners.	Supports learners in the development of personalised and shared learning intentions and success criteria.	Supports learners in the identification of appropriate learning intentions and the development of measurable success criteria.
Goal Setting	States task completion as the goal of the lesson.	States a learning intention as the goal of the lesson.	Considers the learning itself to be the valued goal.	Sets challenging and appropriate learning goals for the group and individual learners.	Models the design of challenging, meaningful goals as a guide for learners, explicitly teaching goal setting.	Guides the co-construction of relevant and challenging learning goals.	Supports learners to establish purpose through the construction of challenging, relevant and measurable individual goals.	Supports learners in the establishment and refinement of academic and personal goals.
Assessment	Evaluates completed tasks.	Evaluates completed work against the stated learning intention.	Has considered how learning may be assessed.	Has determined clearly how success will be evidenced.	Shares examples of success and is transparent about how it is achieved.	Engages in formative assessment practices, supports learners to assess as learning, and teaches the skills of self- and peer-assessment.	Engages learners in self-assessment and evidence collection.	Supports learners to develop a reporting schema to present their evidence of learning against required outcomes.

Table 6.1: Agents to Agency continuum for teachers.

Source: © 2022 by Lee Crockett, Future-Focused Learning Network.

Agents to Agency continuum for learners.

	Level 1 Awareness	Level 2 Connection	Level 3 Remembering	Level 4 Understanding	Level 5 Applying	Level 6 Analysing	Level 7 Evaluating	Level 8 Creating
Learning Foundation	Is unaware of a learning intention beyond the scope of the lesson.	Is aware of the stated learning intention from the curriculum.						Discusses learning with facilitators and mentors, proactively seeking support, guidance and relevant learning opportunities beyond the scope of the classroom or school.
Learning Conversation			Is able to access the learning intention throughout the lesson. Responds to questions to clearly articulate the learning intention.	Responds to questioning by sharing their thoughts, wonderings and critical reflections on the language and meaning of the learning intention. Can clearly articulate the learning intention, responding to questions to explain their understanding of the language and meaning of the learning intention.	Engages in the discussion about the learning intentions, responding from their perspective. Shares prior knowledge through conversation with the group.	Collectively determines the next logical steps in learning. Responds individually to reflective questions, identifying and articulating what they have learned and what should next be learned.	Actively asks questions that drive their learning and seeks feedback or support. Reflects on feedback and applies new thinking to achieve their goals or next steps in learning.	Creates personalised and shared learning intentions and success criteria based on their individualised pathway.
Purpose	Is aware of the stated aim or purpose of the lesson.			Can clearly articulate the purpose, from their perspective, based on their understanding of the learning intention. Understands the learning intention is an endpoint in a series of lessons.		Can identify the lesson objective and can explain how it relates to the learning intentions and success criteria of the unit of learning.	Directs their learning by identifying their pathway to success criteria.	Develops and evolves a personalised learning plan.

Progressions to Self-Directed Learner Agency

Success Criteria	Is unaware of success criteria and how it may be achieved	Can accurately state the success criteria.	Shares ideas and provides input to build group success criteria. Self-assesses diagnostically by connecting to prior knowledge and experience. Understands the success criteria and is able to articulate how they will know they are successful.	Supports the group's learning through the development of shared learning intentions and success criteria.	Creates personalised success criteria relating to individual learning goals. Engages in creating shared success criteria to support the learning of the group.	Creates personalised and shared learning intentions and success criteria based on their individualised pathway.
Goal Setting		Can clearly articulate the learning goals of the group, and or their individual goals as set by the teacher.	Engages in activities to learn and practise goal setting.	Constructs relevant and challenging learning goals.	Creates personalised success criteria relating to individual learning goals.	Sets challenging individual learning and personal goals, ensuring goals, learning plan and purpose are in alignment
Assessment			Self-assesses diagnostically by connecting to prior knowledge and experience.	Reflects on their learning in relation to the learning intentions. Reflect as a group on progress and evidence of learning in relation to success criteria. Is able to self-assess and peer-assess.	Can self-assess, self-report and peer-assess throughout the unit of learning and reflect on their learning individually and as a group.	Plans and develops a reporting schema to produce, collate, self-assess and present evidence of their learning against required outcomes.

Table 6.2: Agents to Agency continuum for learners.

Source: © 2022 Future-Focused Learning Network, Learner Agency Masterclass.

Agents to Agency in Action

The following case studies are written by principals of two schools working with the Future-Focused Learning method: (1) Evelyn Scott School in Canberra and (2) Lalor Primary School in Melbourne. These schools have already begun applying the Agents to Agency process and are seeing immediate results in their students.

Case Study: Evelyn Scott School

By Jackie Vaughan, Principal
Evelyn Scott School

Evelyn Scott School is a brand-new school located in the heart of a new suburb in Canberra, ACT. We began operations in 2021 with approximately 180 children from preschool to Year 5. We are slowly growing each year as families move into our surrounding suburbs, and this year, our second year of operation, we have 300 children from preschool to Year 6. In 2023, we will extend our school to include our senior campus with approximately one hundred young people. The new senior campus completes our P–10 school, which has the capacity to cater for up to 1200 young people across seven impressive buildings.

As the foundation principal, I was fortunate to have been able to work with the architects and builders during the construction phase. The contemporary architecture ensures that the school is purpose-built for future-focused learning (FFL). We have embedded an FFL continuum across the school, spanning play-based learning in the preschool, inquiry learning in the primary school and a project-based learning approach in the high school.

Our vision was strong and clear right from the beginning: to co-create a contemporary and connected school with our community. A P–10 school done well means a robust sense of belonging for children and young people, with minimal transitions and investment in early interventions.

FFL is an academically rigorous teaching and learning framework that provides direction and clarity for all teaching staff. The ACT Future of Education strategy provides the authorising environment for the work that we do at our school, and the shifts of practice (see Crockett, 2019) deliver the road map. Of the many things that the leadership team implemented during the foundation year, the learning model was by far the most significant.

Progressions to Self-Directed Learner Agency

We needed a framework that was going to serve us well from preschool through to Year 10, something that was flexible and explicit so that teachers were able to be creative but within very clear boundaries.

Our teachers are led capably by an FFL executive coach, who has developed expertise since 2021, and her modelling and coaching have meant that we have gained momentum. This year the most successful implementation has been how the FFL PLCs have been structured. We have established vertical PLCs, which are led by our FFL executive coach, and we strictly adhere to the process. Teachers work through a series of challenges and post their results, reflections and feedback in the Future-Focused Learning Network (FFLN). Planning and reflection occur within the PLCs. This time is valued and sacred, and highly productive. From a principal's perspective, the visibility across the school is priceless, as I am able to see what is happening in classrooms from my office.

We have streamlined our professional learning so that teachers do not become confused by the layering effect of too many ideas and strategies. We invest in masterclasses accredited by the ACT's Teacher Quality Institute, and the leadership team models transparency by posting frequently in the FFLN, engaging in the masterclasses and trusting the process. A milestone for our school occurred at the end of Term 2 this year when every teacher posted their recording of Lesson Zero. The ability to post comments and feedback directly to the teachers and share ideas with local, national and international colleagues makes the FFLN a uniquely collaborative, positive and effective digital platform.

Our leadership team has access to Lee Crockett, the founder, and Kathleen Baker-Brown, the director of the FFLN, and the coaching processes keep us accountable and on track. The destination, milestones and footsteps procedure has guided our way of completing 'executive sprints' and has allowed us to move through significant pieces of work without drifting. A new school brings many challenges and complexities, and this process has ensured a genuine sense of efficiency and accomplishment for our team.

The Future Fluencies have provided us with an explicit way to teach essential skills such as problem-solving, collaboration and creativity (Crockett & Churches, 2017). We intend to create a leadership program in 2023 where we train our senior students to use solution fluency to resolve conflict as peer mediators.

We have started to collect qualitative and quantitative data to track our progress. We need sophisticated ways to measure our strategic priorities:

1. Build learners' capacity to solve problems and be critical and creative thinkers and self-directed learners (FFL).

2. Develop learners' belonging and connection to the school (wellbeing).

Early indications are very positive, and we are encouraged by the feedback from our families and learners. Figure 6.2 shows the results from our most recent learner survey from kindergarten to Year 6. The percentages are learners who strongly agreed with the statement.

Evelyn Scott School

I have a say in how I learn — 87%

I understand Learning Intentions — 83%

Learning Intentions are helpful to my learning — 88%

I set goals for my own learning — 95%

I know what successful learning looks like — 93%

Source: © 2022 by Evelyn Scott School. Used with permission.
Figure 6.2: Percentage of Evelyn Scott School students in K–6 who strongly agree with the statements.

Our teachers, support staff and administrative staff all use the FFLN and have benefited from the highly collaborative culture that we have built together. We are still in the beginning stages of our journey, but it is fair to say that we have enjoyed a strong start. Our commitment to future-focused learning has meant that our approach is *built in* rather than *bolt on*. We continue to work on strengthening our practice in partnership with Lee Crockett and the FFLN.

Case Study: Lalor Primary School

By Trevor Robinson, Principal
Lalor Primary School

When I first heard Lee speak about inquiry learning, I instantly knew that this was the path Lalor Primary School needed to go down. Lalor Primary School is in the outer northern suburbs of Melbourne, Victoria, and has a very high socioeconomic disadvantage and considerable barriers to learning, with 70 per cent of our students speaking a language other than English at home. Before engaging with Lee, we used an off-the-shelf inquiry solution. After working with this generic program for some time, it became obvious that we needed a change.

Since switching to future-focused learning, the shift in the pedagogical practice at Lalor Primary School has been significant. Moving from traditional timetabled structures such as English in the morning, mathematics after recess and inquiry after lunch to a school where all students have destinations, milestones and footsteps has been transformational. The learning intentions of our students are now aligned with curriculum achievement standards, have success criteria based on Bloom's revised taxonomy and are co-constructed with the learners. This ensures differentiation of the learning intention based on individual requirements and, therefore, a high rate of success. The questions posed are of high quality and are integrated into the broader learning of our classrooms. Students are allowed time to explore content before a lesson or unit of work is started, which enables every student to know where they are, where they are going and what they need to do to get there. As a result, my staff have moved from long-term planning to creating short-term, adaptable plans explicitly based on the current needs of students.

So often, schools change at a glacial pace, but we have achieved so much in a short time. Amazingly, our moment of glory came during extensive periods of lockdown due to COVID-19. While other schools struggled with remote learning, our staff professionally thrived in the unfamiliar remote environment as a result of the participation and implementation of future-focused learning masterclasses. As a result, our students were engaged and learning progressed during this period.

Our students' growth in mathematics is now four times greater than the average benchmark growth, and their reading growth is 2.5 times greater than the norm. Our NAPLAN data for Year 3 now exceeds the state average in all areas.

How did we get here? To answer this, I will refer to our five agreements (see Crockett, 2019). We stayed curious and courageous and trusted the process and each other (after all, how could we expect our learners to be curious and courageous if we were not?). We dived into the masterclasses and asked questions. We shared and connected, not just with one another but with educators across the Future-Focused Learning Network. When we encountered problems, we reframed them as possibilities (What could this look like? How could this be done?). This reframing created a positive culture that flowed to our students.

What excites me the most as a principal is that we have only just begun to scratch the surface of what we and our learners are capable of achieving. I encourage everybody to start this journey and see where it might lead.

The Future-Focused Learning Network

The Future-Focused Learning Network has existed as a virtual, distributed team based in Canada, Japan, Australia and Dubai for over fifteen years, long before remote work was an accepted method. As a result, we could not have been better prepared for the COVID-19 pandemic. For years, clients in Dubai and Australia have wanted to connect with others doing this work. I recognised that for professional learning to be successful, I needed to be connected to all my schools and the individual teachers to answer their questions and support their growth. One-day workshops on a pupil-free day are more like professional entertainment than professional learning.

For this reason, I created the Future-Focused Learning Network, a global professional learning network. It is a community of professionals who share your passion, and we make it easy for you to find each other and start talking and learning with and from each other. One of the common requests I would field from teachers at a new school was if they could see lessons and videos from others doing this work. In the case study from Evelyn Scott School, principal Jackie Vaughan mentioned that all the teachers had recently completed recording and sharing a Lesson Zero. Imagine the potential of accessing a masterclass over a thousand others have completed, posting their responses to the challenges and their videos of Lesson Zero. To see the work of a thousand other teachers and to be able to ask questions and seek feedback is a rare opportunity.

When lockdowns began, our work with our clients didn't change; we have always been primarily virtual. This enabled us to continue to support teachers and schools as they struggled with the demands of transitioning to remote learning. Evelyn Scott School and Lalor Primary School, both of which have shared case studies in this book, were in the early stages of working with me when lockdowns began. It is important to note that the successes they describe happened during the lockdown and that, because of border closures, I never physically visited either school. All our work was remote. Yet, because of the connections and posts their teachers shared in the Future-Focused Learning Network, I knew all their staff and their work very well. When visiting for the first time, they showed me things we had discussed in the network and the conversation was a natural continuation of our ongoing work.

As you've read this book and the ideas I have put forth, you may have wished you could connect with others doing this work or ask me a question directly. To thank you for purchasing this book, I want to make this possible for you. I invite you to join the Future-Focused Learning Network and access all the resources and masterclasses, including the learning intentions masterclass, on an exclusive thirty-day trial. Hopefully, you find value in connecting with so many of your colleagues who are doing exceptional. The link in figure 6.3 (page 126) will give you free individual access; if you would like to arrange access for your whole school or have other questions, please email me directly at hello@futurefocusedlearning.net.

There's no substitute for LIVE human connection. And those connections happen in the Future-Focused Learning Network, avoiding the privacy concerns of social media.

- Livestreamed events
- Live sessions and meetings
- Personal event calendar
- Group chats
- Exclusive communities of practice
- Masterclasses

Join now for free: futurefocusedlearning.net/agentstoagency

Figure 6.3: Invitation to join the Future-Focused Learning Network.

Conclusion

Source: © 2022 by Daigo Ozawa. Used with permission.
Figure C.1: Ensō (円相), drawn by Daigo Ozawa (小澤 大吾), Jushoku of Hakusan Tokozenji Temple (白山 東光禅寺 住職).

In Zen practice, an ensō (円相), which means *circle aspect*, is drawn in a single, swift, expressive stroke (see figure C.1). Drawing ensō is a spiritual practice of self-realisation called *hitsuzendō* (筆禅道), or *the way of Zen through brush*.

Once drawn, it is left unaltered and exists as a glimpse of the character of the practitioner and the context of its creation at that moment in time. The minimalism of ensō itself symbolises many things, everything and nothing.

Usually the circle is incomplete in acceptance of the truth of the incompletion and impermanence of all things and in appreciation of the beauty of imperfection. It is a beginning, an ending and a new beginning in an endless loop.

There is a sublime simplicity (kanso, 簡素) to this practice; there is only a brush, ink and paper. If you have these, you have everything and need only connect them. In reality this is very difficult, and there is much more occurring. However, everything else beyond brush, ink and paper is the complexity we bring to the practice. Such is with all things in life.

Before we even pick up the brush, a voice is already crying out, 'How much ink should I use? How hard should I press? Where should I begin? What if it's not perfect? What if I make a mistake? I've never been good at drawing! What will people think of me?' And though it is completed in an instant, judgments, criticisms and emotions arise before it is even finished: 'I knew it wouldn't be round! It's not in the middle! I ran out of ink! It's too fat on one side! I should have been more prepared! It looks like a child drew it! What does everyone think? I'm so embarrassed!'

As a practitioner, you become aware of these thoughts, doubts and criticisms and have the opportunity to reflect on their significance. This is why it is a practice of self-realisation. No one else is speaking these things; they are not from your true self but your ego.

The ensō never criticises that it is not round enough, the paper never complains of too much pressure, the brush never moans over a lack of ink and the ink never protests that it is too thin. Opposite us, they all exist in acceptance and non-judgment.

Every time you draw an ensō, it is different. Different thoughts, different experiences and a different ensō bear witness to the moment. Not better, just different. There is no perfection to attain, yet it was perfect in the moment that was, so … let it go and begin again.

Lesson Zero and the shift from agents to agency are the same. Sublime in its simplicity, there are just the learning intentions, the success criteria and the learners. If you have these, you have everything and need only connect them and have the courage to stand aside. Everything beyond the learning intentions, success criteria and the learners is the complexity we bring to

Conclusion

the practice through illusions such as apprehension, uncertainty and fear. In doing so we make it about us, not the learners and their learning.

It is not easy. It takes great courage just to begin, and doing so is victory. It is a beginning, an ending and a new beginning in an endless loop.

Every time you engage in Lesson Zero, it is different. Different learners, different experiences and different learning bear witness to the moment. Not better, just different. There is no perfection to attain, yet it was perfect in the moment that was, so … let it go.

Set your concerns aside, recognise them for the illusions they are and breathe.

Now … let us begin.

References

ACT Education Directorate. (2018). *The Future of Education: An ACT Education Strategy for the Next Ten Years—First Phase Implementation*. Accessed at www.education.act.gov.au/__data/assets/pdf_file/0015/1231080/Future-Of-Education-Final-Strategy_Web.pdf on December 5, 2022.

ACT Education Directorate. (2021). *Future of Education First Phase Implementation Evaluation Report*. Accessed at www.education.act.gov.au/__data/assets/pdf_file/0009/1763460/First-Phase-Evaluation-Report.pdf on December 5, 2022.

ACT Education Directorate. (2022). *Future of Education: An ACT Education Strategy for the Next Ten Years—Phase 2 Implementation Plan*. Accessed at www.education.act.gov.au/__data/assets/pdf_file/0004/1957630/REC21-55028-Attachment-B-FoE-Phase-2-Implementation-Plan.pdf on December 5, 2022.

Almeida, P. A. (2012). Can I ask a question? The importance of classroom questioning. *Procedia-Social and Behavioral Sciences*, *31*, 634–638.

Anderson, L. W., & Krathwohl, D. (Eds.). (2001). *A Taxonomy for Learning, Teaching, and Assessing: A Revision of Bloom's Taxonomy of Educational Objectives*. New York: Longman.

Arslan, M. (2006). The role of questioning in the classroom. *Hasan Ali Yücel Eğitim Fakültesi Dergisi*, *2*, 81–103.

Bandura, A., Freeman, W. H., & Lightsey, R. (1999). Self-efficacy: The exercise of control. *Journal of Cognitive Psychotherapy*, *13*(2), 158–166.

Bates, A. W. (2015). *Teaching in a Digital Age: Guidelines for Designing Teaching and Learning*. Canada: Tony Bates Associates Ltd.

Blaschke, L. M., Bozkurt, A., & Cormier, D. (2021). Learner agency and the learner-centred theories for online networked learning and learning ecologies. In S. Hase & L. M. Blaschke (Eds.), *Unleashing the Power of Learner Agency* (pp. 41–51). EdTech Books.

Blishen, E. (1969). *The School That I'd Like* (1st ed.). United Kingdom: Penguin Books.

Carpenter, J. P., & Pease, J. S. (2013). Preparing students to take responsibility for learning: The role of non-curricular learning strategies. *Journal of Curriculum and Instruction*, *7*(2), 38–55.

Chuter, C. (2020). The role of agency in learning. *The Education Hub*. Accessed at https://theeducationhub.org.nz/agency/ on August 13, 2022.

Crichton, H., & McDaid, A. (2016). Learning intentions and success criteria: Learners' and teachers' views. *Curriculum Journal*. Accessed at https://doi.org/10.1080/09585176.2015.1103278 on December 5, 2022.

Crockett, L. (2019). *Future-Focused Learning: 10 Essential Shifts of Everyday Practice*. Bloomington, IN: Solution Tree Press.

Crockett, L., & Churches, A. (2017). *Mindful Assessment: The 6 Essential Fluencies of Innovative Learning*. Bloomington, IN: Solution Tree Press.

Crockett, L., Jukes, I., & Churches, A. (2011). *Literacy Is Not Enough: 21st-Century Fluencies for the Digital Age*. Thousand Oaks, CA: Corwin Press.

Crowe, M., & Stanford, P. (2010). Questioning for quality. *The Delta Kappa Gamma Bulletin*, 76(4), 36–41.

Dewey, J. (1986). Experience and education. *The Educational Forum*, 50(3), 241–252.

Doran, G. T. (1981). There's a SMART way to write management's goals and objectives. *Management Review*, 70(11), 35–36.

Estrapala, S., & Reed, D. K. (2019). Goal-setting instruction: A step-by-step guide for high school students. *Intervention in School and Clinic*, 55(5), 286–293.

Farmer, G. (2020). *Education: Our flawed and outdated system* [capstone project poster presentation]. College Preparatory Academy, University of Nebraska–Lincoln. Accessed at https://digitalcommons.unl.edu/ncpacapstone/134/ on December 19, 2022.

Ferlazzo, L. (2020). The whys & hows of activating students' background knowledge. *Education Week*. Accessed at www.edweek.org/teaching-learning/opinion-the-whys-hows-of-activating-students-background-knowledge/2020/06 on August 20, 2022.

Fisher, D., Frey, N., Amador, O., & Assof, J. (2018). *The Teacher Clarity Playbook, Grades K–12: A Hands-On Guide to Creating Learning Intentions and Success Criteria for Organized, Effective Instruction*. Thousand Oaks, CA: Corwin Press.

Florkowski, R. W., Wiza, A., & Banaszak, E. (2022). The Rogerian student-centered learning approach and the democratization of education. *Polish Sociological Review*, 218(2), 273–287.

Freire, P. (1970). Cultural action for freedom. *Harvard Educational Review*, 476–521

Grainger, P., Steffler, R., de Villiers Scheepers, M. J., Thiele, C., & Dole, S. (2018). Student negotiated learning, student agency and General Capabilities in the 21st century: The DeLorean Project. *The Australian Educational Researcher*, 46(3), 425–447.

Gross, R. (2020). *Psychology: The Science of Mind and Behaviour* (6th ed.). United Kingdom: Hachette.

Hase, S. & Blaschke, L. M. (2021). *Unleashing the Power of Learner Agency*. EdTech Books.

References

Hattie, J. (2008). *Visible Learning: A Synthesis of Over 800 Meta-Analyses Relating to Achievement*. London: Routledge.

Hattie, J. (2012). *Visible Learning for Teachers: Maximizing Impact on Learning*. London: Routledge.

Holahan, C. K. (1988). Relation of life goals at age 70 to activity participation and health and psychological well-being among Terman's gifted men and women. *Psychology and Aging, 3*(3), 286.

Jukes, I., McCain, T., & Crockett, L. (2010). *Living on the Future Edge: Windows on Tomorrow*. Thousand Oaks, CA: Corwin Press.

Knowles, M. S. (1970). *The Modern Practice of Adult Education: Andragogy Versus Pedagogy* (2nd ed.). New York: Association Press.

Ladson-Billings, G. (2011). Is meeting the diverse needs of all students possible? *Kappa Delta Pi Record, 47*(sup1), 13–15.

Lawlor, K. B., & Hornyak, M. J. (2012). SMART goals: How the application of SMART goals can contribute to achievement of student learning outcomes. *Developments in Business Simulation and Experiential Learning, 39*, 259–267.

Locke, E. A. (1996). Motivation through conscious goal setting. *Applied and Preventive Psychology, 5*(2), 117–124.

Locke, E. A., & Latham, G. P. (1990). *A Theory of Goal Setting & Task Performance*. Englewood Cliffs, NJ: Prentice-Hall, Inc.

Locke, E. A., & Latham, G. P. (2002). Building a practically useful theory of goal setting and task motivation: A 35-year odyssey. *American Psychologist, 57*(9), 705–717.

Lunenburg, F. C. (2011). Goal-setting theory of motivation. *International Journal of Management, Business, and Administration, 15*(1), 6–11.

Mäkitalo, A. (2016). On the notion of agency in studies of interaction and learning. *Learning, Culture, and Social Interaction, 10*, 64–67.

Mameli, C., Molinari, L., & Passini, S. (2018). Agency and responsibility in adolescent students: A challenge for the societies of tomorrow. *British Journal of Educational Psychology, 89*(1), 41–56.

Marbeau, V. (1976). Autonomous study by pupils in secondary schools. *Education and Culture, 31*, 14–21.

Merriam-Webster. (n.d.). Autonomy. *Merriam-Webster.com*. Accessed at www.merriam-webster.com/dictionary/autonomy on December 5, 2022.

Morisano, D. (2013). Goal setting in the academic arena. In E. A. Locke & G. P. Latham (Eds.), *New Developments in Goal Setting and Task Performance* (pp. 495–506). New York: Routledge.

Morisano, D., Hirsh, J. B., Peterson, J. B., Pihl, R. O., & Shore, B. M. (2010). Setting, elaborating, and reflecting on personal goals improves academic performance. *Journal of Applied Psychology, 95*(2), 255–264.

National Council for Curriculum and Assessment. (2015). *Focus on Learning: Learning Intentions and Success Criteria*. Accessed at https://ncca.ie/media/1927/assessment-workshop-1_en.pdf on December 5, 2022.

Organisation for Economic Co-operation and Development (OECD). (2019). *OECD Future of Education and Skills 2010: Conceptual Learning Framework—Student Agency for 2030*. Accessed at www.oecd.org/education/2030-project/teaching-and-learning/learning/student-agency/Student_Agency_for_2030_concept_note.pdf on December 5, 2022.

Piaget, J. (1971). *Psychology and Epistemology: Towards a Theory of Knowledge* (A. Rosin, Trans.; 4th ed.). New York: Grossman.

Ralph, M. (2019). *Old Habits Die Hard: How Learning Goals Can Stifle Deeper Learning*. Accessed at https://melanieralph.com/2019/01/04/360/ on August 25.

Richardson, C., & Mishra, P. (2018). Learning environments that support student creativity: Developing the SCALE. *Thinking Skills and Creativity*, 27, 45–54.

Reeve, J., & Tseng, C.-M. (2011). Agency as a fourth aspect of students' engagement during learning activities. *Contemporary Educational Psychology*, 36(4), 257–267.

Schippers, M. C., Morisano, D., Locke, E. A., Scheepers, A. W. A., Latham, G. P., & de Jong, E. M. (2020). Writing about personal goals and plans regardless of goal type boosts academic performance. *Contemporary Educational Psychology*, 60, 101823.

Schoon, I. (2018). *Conceptualising Learner Agency: A Socio-Ecological Developmental Approach*. London: Centre for Learning and Life Chances in Knowledge Economies and Societies.

Schunk, D. H. (2001). *Self-Regulation Through Goal Setting*. Accessed at https://files.eric.ed.gov/fulltext/ED462671.pdf on December 5, 2022.

Shogren, K. A., Garnier Villarreal, M., Lang, K., & Seo, H. (2017). Mediating role of self-determination constructs in explaining the relationship between school factors and postschool outcomes. *Exceptional Children*, 83(2), 165–180.

Smith, K. G., Locke, E. A., & Barry, D. (1990). Goal setting, planning, and organizational performance: An experimental simulation. *Organizational Behavior and Human Decision Processes*, 46(1), 118–134.

Snow, H. (2022). A recipe for success? Pupils' perspectives on learning intentions and success criteria. *Journal of Trainee Teacher Education Research*, 13, 79–102.

State of Victoria Department of Education and Training. (2017). *High Impact Teaching Strategies: Excellence in Teaching and Learning*. Accessed at www.education.vic.gov.au/Documents/school/teachers/support/Expired/0000highimpactteachstrat-expired.pdf on December 5, 2022.

State of Victoria Department of Education and Training. (2019). *Amplify: Empowering Students Through Voice, Agency and Leadership*. Accessed at www.education.vic.gov.au/Documents/school/teachers/teachingresources/practice/Amplify.pdf on December 5, 2022.

References

Stoddart, S. (2021). *The Education System Is Outdated*. Accessed at www.pvhspoint.org/opinion/2021/12/17/the-education-system-is-outdated/ on December 13, 2022.

Stosny, S. (2011). Self-regulation: To feel better, focus on what is most important. *Psychology Today*. Accessed at www.psychologytoday.com/us/blog/anger-in-the-age-entitlement/201110/self-regulation on September 9, 2022.

UK Department for Education and Skills. (2007). *Assessment for Learning: 8 Schools Project Report*. Accessed at https://dera.ioe.ac.uk/7600/1/1f1ab286369a7ee24df53c863a72da97-1.pdf on December 5, 2022.

United Nations Educational, Scientific and Cultural Organization (UNESCO) Institute for Statistics. (n.d.). Dashboards on the global monitoring of school closures caused by the COVID-19 pandemic. *COVID-19 Education Response*. Accessed at https://covid19.uis.unesco.org/global-monitoring-school-closures-covid19/ on December 5, 2022.

Vallance, E. (1974). Hiding the hidden curriculum: An interpretation of the language of justification in nineteenth-century educational reform. *Curriculum Theory Network*, *4*(1), 5–22.

Vaughn, M. (2019). What is student agency and why is it needed now more than ever? *Theory Into Practice*, *59*(2), 109–118.

Vaughn, M. (2020). Student agency in literacy: A systematic review of the literature. *Reading Psychology*, *41*(7), 712–734.

Voogt, J., Erstad, C. D., & Mishra, P. (2013). Challenges to learning and schooling in the digital networked world of the 21st century. *Journal of Computer Assisted Learning*, 29, 403–413.

Wehmeyer, M. L. (2005). Self-determination and individuals with severe disabilities: Re-examining meanings and misinterpretations. *Research and Practice for Persons with Severe Disabilities*, *30*(3), 113–120.

Wenk, L. (2017). The importance of engaging prior knowledge. *Hampshire College Center for Teaching and Learning*. Accessed at https://sites.hampshire.edu/ctl/2017/09/14/the-importance-of-engaging-prior-knowledge/ on December 5, 2022.

Wiggins, G., & McTighe, J. (2005). Understanding by Design. Alexandria, VA: ASCD.

Williams, P. (2017). Student agency for powerful learning. *Knowledge Quest*, *45*(4), 9–15.

Yusuff, K. B. (2018). Does personalized goal setting and study planning improve academic performance and perception of learning experience in a developing setting? *Journal of Taibah University Medical Sciences*, *13*(3), 232–237.

Index

A

academic emphasis domain, 5
ACER tests for reading and mathematics, 44
achievement standards, 65, 123
   see also Australian Curriculum
agency, 11–27
   in education, 12–13
   goal setting and, 90–94
   misconceptions about, 18–22
   outcome of, 5–8, 12
   pedagogy of, 8, 12, 19 77
   role of the teacher in, 13–16
   teacher agents versus learner agency, 16–18, 26
   teacher facilitation of, 20, 24–26, 102
   through destinations, milestones and footsteps, 97–98
   why it matters, 22–24
   see also learner agency
Agents to Agency, progressions on pathway, 101–126
   in action, 120–124
   continuum for learners, 118–119
   continuum for teachers, 116–117
   FFLN, 124–126
   levels, 102, 103–115
   and Zen practice, 127–129
allocation of time, 67, 68, 77

Amplify strategy, Department of Education Victoria, Australia, 3–4, 17
analysing
   Bloom's taxonomy, 53, 102
   Level 6: Agents to Agency, 110–112
analytical questioning skills, 43
applying
   Bloom's taxonomy, 53, 102
   Level 5: Agents to Agency, 108–110
Aristotle, 90
Ashe, A, 65
assessment, diagnostic, 44–45, 74
assessment in goal setting, 94–95, 96–97
Australia and FFLN, 124
Australian Curriculum, 21, 32–33, 41, 56–57, 71
   see also curriculum and learning intentions
autonomy over learning, 12, 16–18, 90
awareness
   and Bloom's revised taxonomy, 102, 103
   Level 1: Agents to Agency, 103–104

B

Baker-Brown, K, 121
barriers to learning, 23, 25, 123
Bates, AW, 13
behavioural engagement domain, 5
being in the moment, 88

best practice, 103
beyond Lesson Zero (Lesson One), 77–79
Blaschke, LM, 11–12
Bloom's revised taxonomy, 21, 52–53, 70–74, 101, 102, 103
Bloom's zoonomy, 21

C

Canada and FFLN, 124
case studies
    Evelyn Scott School, 120–122
    Lalor Primary School, 123–124
    Lesson Zero, 75–76
Churches, A, 23, 71
clarity for successful learning outcomes, 39–41, 90, 98
    see also success criteria
Clarke, S, 35
collaboration fluency, 20–21
components of a learning intention, 41–43
confusion over levels in Bloom's taxonomy, 71, 73–74
connected journey of intentions, learning, 40–41
connection
    and Bloom's revised taxonomy, 102, 103
    Level 2: Agents to Agency, 104–105
content-focused methods, 3
content knowledge, 23
continuum for learners, 118–119
continuum for teachers, 116–117
COVID-19 pandemic, 6–8, 44, 86, 123, 124
creating
    Bloom's taxonomy, 53, 102
    Level 8: Agents to Agency, 113–115
creativity, lifelong learning skills, 24
criteria for success see success criteria
critical concepts, learning intentions, 33
critical thinking capacity, lifelong learning skills, 24

Crockett, L, 16, 23, 25, 71, 121, 122
cross-disciplinary competencies, 24
curiosity and learning, 15, 29
curriculum and learning intentions, 11, 25, 30, 32, 40–41, 43–44, 50
    see also Australian Curriculum

D

Days of Grace: A Memoir (Ashe), 65
Department of Education Victoria, Australia, 3–4, 17, 18, 19, 31, 35
destinations, for learning, 40, 85, 97–98
destinations, milestones and footsteps, 83–98
    and agency, 97–98
    an overview, 85–90
    goal setting and agency, 90–94
    how learners can start setting goals, 94–97
determination of first steps, Lesson Zero, 74–75
Dewey, J, 12
diagnostic assessment, 44–45, 74
Doran, G, 91
Dubai, GEMS Education, 68, 79
Dubai and FFLN, 124

E

Education Directorate, ACT Australia, 4, 16–17, 18
educational pathway, 20
effect sizes and learning, 40, 67–68
Einstein, A, 11
emotional engagement domain, 5
engaging learners, 45
engaging questions, 58–59
ensō in Zen practice, 127–129
essential questions, 51–57
essential understandings, learning intentions, 32–33
essential understandings and essential questions, 55–57

ethical and moral considerations, lifelong learning skills, 24
evaluating
  Bloom's taxonomy, 53, 102
  Level 7: Agents to Agency, 112–113
Evelyn Scott School, ACT, Australia, 21, 120–122, 124, 125
evolving practice, 103

F
facilitation of agency, 20, 24–26, 102
FFLN (Future-Focused Learning Network), 8, 21, 38, 101, 121–122, 124–126
first steps, Lesson Zero, 74–75
footsteps in planning, 86–90, 97–98
Freire, P, 3, 11
Future Fluencies, 121–122
future-focused learning, 51, 120
  see also Evelyn Scott School; Lalor Primary School
Future-Focused Learning (Crockett), 25, 29, 51, 69
Future-Focused Learning Network (FFLN) see FFLN (Future-Focused Learning Network)
future learning, learning intentions, 40–42
Future of Education strategy, Education Directorate ACT, Australia, 4–5, 120

G
GEMS Education, Dubai, 68
General Capabilities, Australian Curriculum, 33
goal setting, self-determination in, 90–91, 94–96
goal setting and agency, 90–94
goal setting and learning intentions, 31, 45, 85
  see also SMART goals

H
Hattie, J, 31, 40, 67, 68
herding questions, 51, 57–62
higher-order thinking skills, 44–45, 52–53, 55, 61, 97
hope, peril of, 3–5

I
independent learners, 3, 8, 15, 25
individual development, 12
individual perspectives, learning intentions, 34
inquiry, learning intentions, 34
intentions of learning see learning intentions
intercultural awareness and understanding, lifelong learning skills, 24
Ionesco, E, 49

J
Japan and FFLN, 124
journey of intentions, learning, 40–41
Jukes, I, 23

K
Knowles, MS, 12

L
Lalor Primary School, Victoria, Australia, 8, 44, 71–73, 123–124, 125
language of the learning intention, 41–42
Lao Tzu, 83
leading questions, 58, 59–60
  learner agency
    progressions to, 101–126
    shift to, 5–8, 15, 26
    and SMART goals, 93–94
    versus teacher agents, 16–18, 26
learner voice concept, 16, 18–22
learning, 12–16, 18–20
  clarity for successful learning outcomes, 39–41, 90, 98
  connected journey of intentions, 40–41
  learning how to learn, 14, 21, 23
  learning in context, 49
  see also barriers to learning
Learning Area Rationales, Australian Curriculum, 32
learning goals
  learners setting goals, 94–97, 97–98
  personal, 31

leaning intentions 2.0, 29–47
    clarity for successful outcomes, 39–41, 90, 98
    destinations and, 40, 97–98
    intentions of learning, 30–31
    learning as a connected journey of intentions, 40–41
    learning intentions and lesson objectives, 32–34, 65
    learning intentions versus lesson objectives, 34–39, 65
    Lesson Zero, 69–70
    unpacking learning intentions, 38, 41–45
    see also success criteria
Learning Intentions Shift of Practice from Early Years to Year 10, 36–37
lesson objectives, 32–39, 65, 97–98
Lesson One (beyond Lesson Zero), 77–79
Lesson Zero, 65–82
    in action, 68–75, 121, 124–125
    and beyond, 77–79
    case study, 75–76
    reminders about, 80–81
    what it is, 66–68
    and Zen practice, 127–129
levels of Agents to Agency, 102, 103, 103–115
levels of Bloom's taxonomy, 53, 71, 73–74
lifelong learning skills, 24, 97
literacy, 12, 21, 23, 43, 44, 45
Literacy Is Not Enough (Crockett et al.), 23
long-term planning, 88, 123
lower-order thinking skills, 50, 52–53

M

McGill University, 93, 97
McTighe, J, 55
meaningful questions, 49
milestones in planning, 86, 97–98
Mindful Assessment (Crockett & Churches), 16, 71, 74, 77
mindfulness practice, 12, 83
misconceptions about agency, 18–22
momentum in learning, 59, 83
Morisano, D, 97

N

NAPLAN (National Assessment Program – Literacy and Numeracy), 45, 124

O

objectives, lesson, 32–39, 65, 97–98
OECD Learning Compass 2030, 19
older students and agency, 21–22
oppression, pedagogy of, 2–3, 8, 11, 12, 19, 21, 66
Out of My Later Years (Einstein), 11

P

passive consumption of knowledge, 14, 15
pathway, Lesson Zero, 75
pathway of Agents to Agency, 102, 102, 103–115
pedagogy of agency, 8, 12, 19 77
pedagogy of the oppressed, 2–3, 8, 11, 12, 19, 21, 22, 66
Pedagogy of the Oppressed (Friere), 11
personal educational pathway, 20
personal responsibility, lifelong learning skills, 24
Piaget, J, 12
planning, to support teams, 84–85, 88–90
Plato, 90
prior knowledge, learning intentions, 41, 45
problem-solving ability, lifelong learning skills, 24
provocation, Lesson Zero, 69
purpose, Lesson Zero, 65, 70
purposeful questioning, 34, 49–63
    how to make questions essential, 51–57
    learner wrangling and herding questions, 57–62
    and learning intentions, 34, 44–45

why this matters, 51
see also questions

Q
questions
    analytical questioning skills, 43–44
    essential questions, 51–57
    herding questions, 51, 57–62
    questioning behaviours, 50
    unpacking of, 43–44

R
remembering
    Bloom's taxonomy, 53, 102
    Level 3: Agents to Agency, 105–106
reminders about Lesson Zero, 80–81
responsibility for learning, 5–8, 13–16, 18–20, 26
return on investment (ROI), time allocation, 68
Robinson, T, 44, 123
role of the teacher, 13–16

S
school improvement plan, 85
self- and peer-assessment, 71
self-assessment in goal setting, 94–95, 96–97
self-determination, 12, 90, 94–96
self-directed learner agency, 12, 101–126
self-regulation in goal setting, 94–95, 96
setting goals, 31, 90–97
78 Important Questions Every Leader Should Ask and Answer (Ionesco), 49
Shakespeare, W, 101
shift responsibility for learning, 5–8, 15, 26
shifts of practice in future-focused learning, 51, 120
simplicity in approach to learning, 98
SMART goals, 91–94
social skills, lifelong learning skills, 24
specificity in essential questions, 53–55
steering questions, 58, 61–62

strategic plans, 84
student agency, 3–5
    see also learner agency
success criteria, 21, 22, 30, 31, 38–39, 65
    Lesson One (beyond Lesson Zero), 77–79
    Lesson Zero, 65, 70–74
    milestones, 88, 97–98
    self-assessment, 94–95, 96–97
    and SMART strategy, 93
    see also clarity for successful learning outcomes
synchronous delivery of content, 7–8

T
The Taming of the Shrew (Shakespeare), 101
Tao Te Ching (Lao Tzu), 83
teacher agents versus learner agency, 16–18, 26
teacher-centred methods, 3, 6
teacher facilitation of agency, 20, 24–26
Teacher Quality Institute (ACT), 121
teaching, focus on teacher/learner, 6
telling to asking, transition, 49
10 shifts of practice in future-focused learning, 51, 120
thinking skills, 44–45, 50, 52–53, 55, 61, 97
time allocation, 67, 68, 77
transactional approach of learning, 24
two-step approach to making questions essential, 52–55

U
understanding
    Bloom's taxonomy, 53, 102
    Level 4: Agents to Agency, 106–108
Understanding by Design (Wiggins & McTighe), 55
University of Glasgow study, 38–39, 68
University of Rotterdam study, 93–94
unpacking learning intentions, 41–45, 69–70, 71
unpacking questions, learning intentions, 43

V
Varkey, S, 68
Vaughan, J, 120, 124
Vaughan, M, 24
verbs and objects, language of the learning intention, 41–43, 44
voice, learner, 16, 18–20

W
WALT (We are learning to), 35
what/why/how of learning, 29–30
Wiggins, G, 55
WILF (What I am looking for), 35
work landscape transformed, 22–23

Y
Year Level Descriptors, Australian Curriculum, 33
Yousafzai, M, 29

Z
Zen practice, 127–129